30-SECOND CINEMA

30-SECOND CINEMA

The 50 most important ideas, genres
and people in the history of movies,
each explained in half a minute

Editor
Pamela Hutchinson

Contributors
Nikki Baughan
Anton Bitel
Phil Hoad
Pamela Hutchinson
Christina Newland
Kelli Weston

Illustrator
Nicky Ackland-Snow

IVY PRESS

First published in the UK in 2019 by
Ivy Press
An imprint of The Quarto Group
The Old Brewery, 6 Blundell Street
London N7 9BH, United Kingdom
T (0)20 7700 6700 **F** (0)20 7700 8066
www.QuartoKnows.com

British Library Cataloguing-in-
Publication Data
A catalogue record for this
book is available from the
British Library.

ISBN: 978-1-78240-549-8

This book was conceived,
designed and produced by
Ivy Press
58 West Street, Brighton BN1 2RA, UK

Publisher **Susan Kelly**
Creative Director **Michael Whitehead**
Editorial Director **Tom Kitch**
Commissioning Editor **Sophie Collins**
Project Editor **Joanna Bentley**
Designer **Ginny Zeal**
Picture Researcher **Katie Greenwood**

Printed in China

10 9 8 7 6 5 4 3 2 1

CONTENTS

INTRODUCTION
Pamela Hutchinson

Cinema is a young and constantly evolving
medium. When the Lumière brothers first demonstrated their invention
to the public in Paris on 28 December 1895, they knew that there was
an appetite for the novelty of moving images, but they feared their
invention had no future. A few months later, a woman called Alice
Guy-Blaché shot the first film with a narrative, *The Cabbage Fairy*.
This, we now know, was the future.

Whether Hollywood blockbusters or amateur documentaries, colourful
cartoons or sociological statements, cinema remains one of our most
powerful tools for telling stories. This book tells stories, too. We tell you
how some film-makers grouped together to form industries, including the
monoliths of Hollywood and Bollywood that were born in the 1910s, and
how many others resisted corporate ties, continuing the pioneer spirit of
the early days. We will share the work of some of the finest and most

*The Lumières may have
called it 'an invention
without a future' but the
moving image has proved
central to the twentieth
and twenty-first centuries,
whether for creating fiction
or recording reality.*

influential film directors, but also the stars – icons such as Marilyn Monroe and Shah Rukh Khan – who came to define whole eras, and the staple genres, such as musicals and westerns, which have evolved alongside the cinema itself.

In the middle of the twentieth century, commercial cinema was shaken by the rise of television and legal challenges to its industry practices. Since then, the story of cinema has been rocked by upheavals, with collectives and individuals reclaiming the cinema for their generations, from the Italian Neorealists in the 1940s to the directors of New Queer Cinema in the 1990s. The technical advances of the late twentieth and early twenty-first centuries have also broken fresh ground, from great leaps in special effects and cinema technology, to a new imagining of the cinema experience itself. Will we soon watch more films alone, immersed in our private virtual-reality headsets, than we do collectively in the cinema?

From the first movie cameras to computer-generated imagery and 4D cinemas, technological advances have driven how we make and view films.

Italian star Marcello Mastroianni plays a frustrated film director in Federico Fellini's Oscar-winning innovative comedy 8½ (1963). It's a classic example of a film in love with the medium itself and of a collaboration between a popular star and an auteur director.

This is a guidebook for helping you explore this shifting landscape. We start your tour at the beginning, in the frontier days of the silent era, and we take you through some of the creative movements that influenced the films you watch today. You'll be introduced to the stars and directors who have made an impact on global cinema, the most popular genres, and the innovators who progressed the art form by reinventing it again and again.

We take a look behind the scenes at the business side of the industry, where the decisions get made and reputations are made and lost. We also encourage you to stray from that path and venture towards experimental works that are unlikely to be screened at your local multiplex.

It is hard to imagine modern cinema without Hollywood, red carpets, blockbusters and megastars, but there is so much more to the movies than that. Since the cinema became a business, financial interests and the preferences of a select few have dictated the films that are most widely distributed and often the people who get to make those films. While we have featured some of the very biggest names in the business on these pages, we also encourage you to step outside the mainstream and meet the people who have used film to capture their own realities or express their own subjective view of the world, the marginalized or esoteric voices that don't make multimillion-dollar deals in Los Angeles.

Cinema can show us imaginary worlds and people, such as in Avatar *(2009), directed by James Cameron.*

Our guidebook may not cover every corner of the cinematic world, but we hope that it will point you in helpful directions – you can look up the films and film-makers that interest you to find the works that inspired them, and the works that they influenced in turn. Each themed chapter also includes a glossary of essential terms, and a profile of a key player, giving you the basics you need to explore film further. It's a journey that will take you to different continents and other eras, to films that don't tell stories in conventional ways or don't tell stories at all. The big screen offers plenty of opportunities to broaden your horizons.

I remember my first steps to becoming a cinephile. The first film that made me realize that cinema was more than just filmed drama was David Lean's *Great Expectations* (1946), which I saw on TV as a bookish child. The first arthouse films I encountered were in the form of a French New Wave double-bill when I was a teenager, while my first silent film was a thrilling but baffling screening of *Un Chien Andalou* (1929) at college. My fellow contributors to this book, all brilliant writers and experts on cinema, are about to share their paths with you, too. Reading around the films we love led us on to more and more discoveries, until we became fearless travellers through cinematic space and time.

Your own journey begins here. Here's your map.

THE BEGINNING

THE BEGINNING
GLOSSARY

Cinématographe Invented by Auguste and Louis Lumière in 1895, this device could both record and project moving images. The name was coined by inventor Léon Bouly for a previous invention and is derived from a Greek phrase meaning 'writing in movement'. The Lumière brothers bought the right to the name for their own creation.

close-up A tightly framed shot, usually of a face. Other types of shot include two-shots, where two figures are shown, medium shots and long shots. Shot-reverse-shot is the name for a pattern of shots showing the alternate perspective of two figures looking at each other.

cross-cutting An editing technique that cuts between simultaneous action in two different spaces, often used to build tension.

German Expressionism Early twentieth-century art movement, encompassing visual arts, literature, theatre, cinema and even architecture, which privileged psychological realism over verisimilitude – mimicry of the real world. Expressionist works are characterized by simple shapes, visible brush strokes, steep angles and deep shadows. The first German Expressionist film was *The Cabinet of Dr Caligari* (1920), followed by many more stylish, angst-ridden classics in the 1920s.

Kinetograph Device invented by Thomas Edison and W. K. L. Dickson in the 1880s, based on Eadweard Muybridge's experiments with photographing movement and using celluloid film, which had been invented by George Eastman. The first Kinetographs could record moving images on film, but not play them back.

Kinetoscope Dickson and Edison's peephole viewing device allowed a single viewer to watch a loop of film, which had been shot on a Kinetograph. The perforations on the edges of the film allowed it to move smoothly in front of the viewing window via sprockets.

Oscar Official nickname for the Academy Awards. The name 'Oscar' was first used in public by Walt Disney in 1932, but there is a dispute over who invented it. Bette Davis claimed in her autobiography that she named the statuette after her first husband, Harmon Oscar Nelson, while others say the Academy's executive secretary Margaret Herrick exclaimed that the figurine looked like her uncle Oscar and the name stuck.

realism This term has two meanings in cinema. Firstly, it is a measure of verisimilitude, or how closely the cinematic image mimics the real world, as in Classical Hollywood cinema. Secondly, it applies to cinema that questions the contrivances that create that illusion: by using only natural light, for example, or by drawing attention to the way that the film is edited.

soundstage A film studio converted for use in shooting sound cinema – complete with microphones and acoustic insulation, and isolated from other sources of noise.

talkie Colloquial term for a sound film: after silent 'movies' came the sound 'talkies'. However, the term 'movies' remains in use for all films, while 'talkie' is used only in fun or to describe early sound films.

trick film Early-cinema term for a film showcasing the era's special effects: fast and slow motion, rewinds, multiple exposures and jump-cut edits that allowed objects to appear and disappear in the frame. All these effects were achieved live, 'in-camera'.

THE INVENTORS

the 30-second feature

It is impossible to name one person as the overall inventor of the cinema. Not only do historians dispute who was first, but also several different inventions contributed to the making of moving-picture cameras and projectors. In Leeds, England, a Frenchman called Louis Le Prince recorded short scenes on paper in 1888. These look very much like films, but were too fragile to withstand repeated projection. In 1891, in New Jersey, USA, prolific inventor Thomas Edison worked with photographer W. K. L. Dickson to invent the Kinetograph motion picture camera and the Kinetoscope peephole viewer. Although these devices allowed people to shoot and screen films, they could only be viewed by one person at a time. In France, in 1895, brothers Auguste and Louis Lumière created the Cinématographe, a machine that could both record moving pictures and project them onto a screen. This was first shown to the public on 28 December 1895 at the Grand Café in Paris – an event considered by most to be the first cinema screening. More debatable is the popular legend that at subsequent shows, audiences fled in terror from a film of a train moving forward towards the camera.

RELATED FEATURE
See also
EARLY CINEMA
page 16

3-SECOND TRAILER
The cinema had many inventors from across the globe, all rushing to realize the dream of making moving pictures.

3-MINUTE SEQUEL
Even the inventors of the Cinématographe couldn't imagine the development of the cinema. Louis Lumière famously called the machine 'an invention without a future'. We can think about the history of cinema in the early years as the period in which people understood how to turn moving photographs into an art form of their own – with stories and spectacle and by using the special qualities of film to their best advantage.

3-SECOND BIOGRAPHIES
LOUIS LE PRINCE
1841–90
Brilliant French inventor who disappeared in mysterious circumstances aged 49

THOMAS EDISON
1847–1931
US businessman and inventor who developed the light bulb and phonograph as well as motion pictures

AUGUSTE & LOUIS LUMIÈRE
1862–1954 & 1864–1948
French owners of a photographic factory who invented the Cinématographe

30-SECOND TEXT
Pamela Hutchinson

Inventors around the world scrambled to make pictures move in the nineteenth century. Were the audiences terrified, or entranced?

EARLY CINEMA

the 30-second feature

The early years of cinema were a time of experimentation and adventure. The first film-makers made distant worlds visible to untravelled audiences and invented new, fantastical landscapes on the screen. Many early films were 'actualities' – short films offering snapshots of everyday life or important occasions. These films have an enduring appeal, offering glimpses of lost worlds and historical figures. Film-makers such as Georges Méliès from France and Segundo de Chomón from Spain combined stage effects and in-camera edits to make magical 'trick films' that continue to delight and baffle audiences with their inventiveness and surreal humour. In the early twentieth century, directors were also beginning to explore ideas of narrative, editing together scenes in order to tell stories, and in Edwin S. Porter's landmark western *The Great Train Robbery* (1903), cross-cutting between action in two different places to build suspense. In the early years, films were shown in fairs, carnivals, theatres, music halls and shop-front nickelodeons. There would most likely have been musical accompaniment at each screening, from a solo musician. The first film audiences watched movies projected on sheets, while sitting on uncomfortable benches in noisy rooms. Purpose-built cinemas with comfortable seating were yet to come.

RELATED FEATURES
See also
THE INVENTORS
page 14

SILENT CINEMA
page 18

3-SECOND BIOGRAPHIES
GEORGES MÉLIÈS
1861–1938
Stage illusionist turned film-maker who pioneered in-camera special effects such as superimpositions and stop-motion vanishing acts

EDWIN S. PORTER
1870–1941
Film-maker at the Edison company; among the first to use close-ups and cross-cutting

ALICE GUY-BLACHÉ
1873–1968
Director of the first fiction film, *The Cabbage Fairy* (1896), and later epics such as *The Life of Christ* (1906)

30-SECOND TEXT
Pamela Hutchinson

Gorgeous and gruesome uses of hand-applied colour in Georges Méliès's 1902 film **A Trip to the Moon.**

3-SECOND TRAILER
Film pioneers travelled far and wide and experimented with genre, storytelling, special effects and colour to create the new medium of cinema.

3-MINUTE SEQUEL
In this period, prestigious films benefited from beautifully applied colour – either added freehand or using stencils. One defining image of the era is the famous scene from Méliès's 1902 science-fiction film *A Trip to the Moon*, which combined trick effects, narrative and hand-painted colour. The man in the moon grimaces as a rocket ship of earthlings lands smack in his eye, spurting crimson gore.

SILENT CINEMA

the 30-second feature

In the 1910s and 1920s, cinema began to look much like it does today, apart from the silence – a successful method of recording synchronized sound with pictures had not yet arrived. While Europe was caught up in the First World War, the American film industry, newly centred in Hollywood, began to dominate. The US industry produced copious dramatic feature films and slapstick comedies such as those by Charlie Chaplin and Buster Keaton. Hollywood made increasingly elaborate, nuanced pictures including King Vidor's *The Crowd* (1928), Clarence Brown's *Flesh and the Devil* (1926) and F. W. Murnau's *Sunrise* (1927). After the war, German cinema entered a period of great creativity, with famed directors Ernst Lubitsch (*Madame Dubarry*, 1919), Murnau (*Nosferatu*, 1922) and Fritz Lang (*Metropolis*, 1927), as expressionism gave way to an emphasis on realism. French studios produced artistic, ambitious films, such as the epic *Napoléon* by Abel Gance (1927). Also in France, Danish director Carl Th. Dreyer made the masterpiece *The Passion of Joan of Arc* (1928). In Britain, Alfred Hitchcock made his first thrillers in silence, including *The Lodger* (1927) and *Blackmail* (1929). Films were now shown in lavishly decorated purpose-built cinemas, with comfortable seating and room for several musicians.

3-SECOND TRAILER
In the silent cinema era, the film industry and cinematic creativity boomed, with dramatic feature films, realistic movies and ambitious epics.

3-MINUTE SEQUEL
The 1920s was an especially fertile period for cinema around the world. As in the USA and Europe, the Russian and Japanese movie industries made films of enduring quality and appeal. Sadly, 80 per cent of all silent movies are thought to be lost, so there is much we will never see. But there is always hope: every year, new discoveries of lost films improve our appreciation of the era.

RELATED FEATURES
See also
CHARLIE CHAPLIN
page 50

GERMAN EXPRESSIONISM
page 94

SOVIET MONTAGE
page 96

3-SECOND BIOGRAPHIES
F. W. MURNAU
1888–1931
Acclaimed German film director who was signed by Fox in 1926; he died aged just 42 in a car crash and never made a talkie

CARL TH. DREYER
1889–1968
Danish director who transitioned to sound cinema with the haunting part-talkie horror *Vampyr* (1932)

30-SECOND TEXT
Pamela Hutchinson

From slapstick to tragedy, silent cinema had many moods.

1875
Born in Oldham County, Kentucky, USA

1907
Enters the film business as a writer and actor

1908
Directs his first film, *The Adventures of Dollie*, followed by more than 400 more for the Biograph Company

1915
The Birth of a Nation prompts protests across the USA

1919
Co-founds United Artists; makes *Broken Blossoms* (1919), *Way Down East* (1920) and *Orphans of the Storm* (1921)

1924
Leaves United Artists

1931
Makes final film, *The Struggle*, about alcoholism; widely considered a failure

1936
Awarded an honorary Oscar

1940
New York's Museum of Modern Art hosts a retrospective of all his major works

1948
Dies at Temple Hospital in Hollywood of a cerebral haemorrhage

D. W. GRIFFITH

'Remember how small the world was before I came along? I brought it all to life: I moved the whole world onto a 20-foot screen.' D. W. Griffith, who directed more than 500 films between 1908 and 1931, is one of the most famous, and notorious, figures of the silent era. He is rightly celebrated as a cinema pioneer, although he has been falsely credited with such key inventions as the close-up and the narrative feature film. His triumphs are tarnished, however, by the objectionable racism of his landmark film, Reconstruction epic *The Birth of a Nation* (1915).

Griffith was born in Kentucky, USA in 1875, the son of a former Confederate Army general. Growing up, he absorbed tales of the South along with his passion for theatre and Victorian literature. As an adult, Griffith was an actor, mostly in touring companies. In 1907, he entered the film business in New York. The Biograph Company soon put the actor in charge of its entire production, directing one-reelers with cameraman G. W. 'Billy' Bitzer. Griffith coached his actors to give naturalistic performances more suited to the camera than the stage, and his characters, played by a company that included Mary Pickford and Lillian Gish, had convincing psychological depths. He worked across all genres, but specialized in 'race-to-the-rescue' climaxes.

Working in Hollywood in the 1910s, Griffith began to make feature-length films, including *The Birth of a Nation*, his adaptation of Thomas Dixon's play *The Clansman*. Protested against by the National Association for the Advancement of Colored People and used as a recruitment tool by the Ku Klux Klan, this film demonstrated the centrality of cinema to American culture in the most terrifying way. Griffith's next film was even more ambitious, but failed to make the same impact at the box office. *Intolerance* (1916) has four narrative strands set centuries apart, giant sets and another famous race climax.

In 1919, Griffith joined Charlie Chaplin, Mary Pickford and Douglas Fairbanks to form the United Artists (UA) studio, and made *Broken Blossoms*, a stunning melodrama with Gish as a Cockney waif. However, while Griffith made some excellent films in the early 1920s, he failed to earn enough to get a return on his investment in UA. Over the rest of the decade, Griffith's films fell out of fashion and he drank heavily. He died in 1948, by no means forgotten, but fallen far from the grace he once enjoyed.

Pamela Hutchinson

THE COMING OF SOUND

the 30-second feature

'Wait a minute, wait a minute, you ain't heard nothin' yet.' With those words, singer Al Jolson is said to have changed cinema for ever. This is his first speech in the movie *The Jazz Singer*, released in the USA in October 1927. While many previous films had experimented with sound in various forms, this Warner Bros musical was the first movie with a full-length recorded, synchronized soundtrack: not just incidental tunes but songs and speech too. With the studio's heavy backing, and Jolson's popularity, this film became a hit and the tipping point for a sea change in the industry. To join the 'talkie' revolution, studios had to build new soundstages and overcome the difficulties of recording sound, while cinemas had to install electric speaker systems. This process took place over a few years, and once the industry had invested in sound, there was no going back to silent movies. While film crews grappled with the new technology, movies initially lost some of the elegant expressiveness of the late silent era. Yet by the 1930s, comedies included smart, snappy dialogue; crime films such as *Scarface* (1932) featured barrages of noisy gunfire; and the movie musical was born, celebrating visual and melodious splendour, an invention spectacularly depicted in the 1952 comedy *Singin' in the Rain*.

RELATED FEATURES
See also
MUSICALS
page 38

STUDIO SYSTEM
page 116

3-SECOND BIOGRAPHY
AL JOLSON
1886–1950
American actor, singer and comedian famous for his blackface minstrel routines and the hit songs *Swanee* and *My Mammy*

30-SECOND TEXT
Pamela Hutchinson

Audiences flocked to see popular entertainer Al Jolson sing – and speak – on screen, and the talkie revolution began.

GENRES

GENRES
GLOSSARY

cel Short for celluloid, cel refers to transparent plastic sheets used in traditional, hand-drawn animation.

Cinématographe Invented by Auguste and Louis Lumière in 1895, this device could both record and project moving images. The name was coined by inventor Léon Bouly for a previous invention and is derived from a Greek phrase meaning 'writing in movement'. The Lumière brothers bought the right to the name for their own creation.

Direct Cinema Documentary genre inspired by photojournalism that capitalized on lightweight cameras and better sound-recording equipment to capture life 'in the raw'. In Direct Cinema, the camera and the film-maker are completely unobtrusive.

found footage A sub-genre in which all or part of the movie is presented as discovered film or video, often with authentically shaky camerawork and naturalistic acting. It's especially popular in horror: *The Blair Witch Project* (1999) is a famous example.

genre Category of films, such as western, musical and thriller, all with their own tropes and often sub-genres too. Commercial cinema is more likely to slot neatly into a genre than arthouse fare.

Golden Age of Hollywood Roughly defined as 1927–63, the period when US cinema was the dominant form of popular mass entertainment, produced using the processes of the studio system, with techniques and aesthetics now described by the umbrella term Classical Hollywood cinema. With hindsight, critics have discovered much to admire, including touches of individualism and brilliance.

Hays Code The Motion Picture Production Code, informally named after author Will H. Hays, was Hollywood's first attempt at self-censorship. Technically voluntary, the code gave guidelines for the depictions of topics including sex, profanity, violence, crime and drugs.

New Hollywood Also called the American New Wave, this movement dates roughly from the late 1960s to the early 1980s, when a generation of US film-makers were influenced by world and arthouse cinema.

Oscar Official nickname for the Academy Awards. The name Oscar was first used in public by Walt Disney in 1932, but there is a dispute over who invented it. Bette Davis claimed that she named the statuette after her first husband, Harmon Oscar Nelson, while others say the Academy's executive secretary Margaret Herrick exclaimed that the figurine looked like her uncle Oscar and the name stuck.

rom-com Popular abbreviation for romantic comedy, which has shifted to mean specifically a light, female-oriented film, often denigrated as formulaic. Conversely, romantic comedies directed by male auteurs transcend the label.

slasher Horror film in which a mysterious villain murders a group of young people, especially women, one-by-one. Traditionally, the last one left alive is a virgin known as 'the final girl'. The psychopathic villains, usually male, often recur in sequels and franchises.

studio system During the Golden Age of Hollywood, major studios thrived thanks to a combination of factory-inspired production methods, using creative staff on long-term contracts, and vertical integration, that is, the ownership of distribution and exhibition. Anti-trust laws were first used to challenge this monopoly in the late 1940s, leading to the demise of the system by the 1960s.

talkie Colloquial term for a sound film: after silent 'movies' came the sound 'talkies'. However, the term 'movies' remains in use for all films, while 'talkie' is used only in fun or to describe early sound films.

Technicolor Process for reproducing colour on film, first used in 1916, appearing in several different iterations since and still used today. In the late 1930s Technicolor's highly saturated hues were popular in musicals, animation and adventure films.

torture porn Extreme form of horror film, which focuses in detail and for extended periods on bodily mutilation and torture.

uncanny valley Aesthetic concept explaining why objects that look nearly, but not quite, human produce feelings of disgust or eeriness in onlookers.

Universal Monsters Name for the horror, sci-fi and suspense movies made by the Universal studio from the 1920s to the 1950s, often starring Bela Lugosi, Boris Karloff, or Lon Chaney Sr or Jr.

WESTERNS

the 30-second feature

The legends of the American Old West were fresh memories when the movies began, and outlaw tales transferred perfectly to the screen: clearly defined heroes and villains engaged in shoot-outs, robberies and saloon brawls. John Ford, the master of the genre, began making westerns in 1913 and continued until 1964, including in his output *Stagecoach* (1939), the break-out role for cowboy star John Wayne. Over the years, the western genre has engaged in increasingly complex explorations of the American relationship to law and order, violence and race. *The Searchers* (1956) examines the genre's thoughtless hatred for Native Americans. In *High Noon* (1952), Gary Cooper's sheriff puts small-town cowardice to shame. By the 1960s, directors Sam Peckinpah (*The Wild Bunch*, 1969) and Sergio Leone reconsidered the genre with even more gratuitous violence and cynicism. Italian director Leone invented the 'spaghetti western' and popularized Clint Eastwood as the Man with No Name in *The Good, the Bad, and the Ugly* (1968). The genre has continued to progress into the twenty-first century, including revisionist westerns such as Andrew Dominik's *The Assassination of Jesse James by the Coward Robert Ford* (2007) and Quentin Tarantino's *The Hateful Eight* (2016).

3-SECOND TRAILER
With its memorable heroes and villains, the wild history of the American West provides film-makers with a rich source of material to celebrate and critique.

3-MINUTE SEQUEL
The 1950s were widely seen as a 'golden age' for American westerns, featuring not only some of John Ford's finest works, but also films such as Howard Hawks' *Rio Bravo* (1959), a riposte to *High Noon*, and George Stevens' *Shane* (1953) starring Alan Ladd as a mysterious lone gunslinger. Actor James Stewart also starred as a dark anti-hero in a series of westerns by director Anthony Mann, which included *Winchester '73* (1950) and *The Man from Laramie* (1955).

RELATED FEATURES
See also
SILENT CINEMA
page 18

NEW HOLLYWOOD
page 108

THE STUDIO SYSTEM
page 116

3-SECOND BIOGRAPHIES
JOHN WAYNE
1907–79
The most famous cowboy actor of Hollywood's Golden Age; star of westerns including *Stagecoach* and *The Searchers*

SAM PECKINPAH
1925–84
New Hollywood film-maker nicknamed 'Bloody Sam', who made ultra-violent westerns in the 1960s and 1970s

30-SECOND TEXT
Christina Newland

Clint Eastwood and John Wayne represent two very different types of hero in the western genre.

ROM-COMS

the 30-second feature

3-SECOND TRAILER
The rom-com is the most enduring of film genres, thanks to its ability to find humour in the emotional (and sometimes physical) turmoils of love.

3-MINUTE SEQUEL
The origins of the romantic comedy go back before the birth of cinema. The godfather of the universally accessible rom-com is undoubtedly William Shakespeare, whose plays often involve a couple having an instant attraction but having to overcome obstacles to secure their happy ending. Many of his works have been adapted for the screen, often multiple times, including his romantic comedies *A Midsummer Night's Dream* and *Much Ado About Nothing*.

One of the first films shown to the public was *The Kiss*, an 18-second canoodle made by William Heise in 1896, and film-makers have been fascinated by matters of the heart ever since. Finding humour in the complexities of love, the romantic comedy has endured not just because of its universality, but because it has evolved to meet the expectations of the day. Many silent films, such as *My Best Girl* (1927), could be termed rom-coms, but the genre hit its stride with the dawn of talkies. The following two decades were the golden age of screwball comedies such as *The Awful Truth* (1937), *Bringing Up Baby* (1938) or *The Philadelphia Story* (1940), in which men and women traded rapid-fire witticisms while falling in and out of love. In the 1950s, rom-coms became more risqué, with films such as *Some Like It Hot* (1959) and *The Seven Year Itch* (1955), directed by Billy Wilder and starring Marilyn Monroe. The 1990s was a second boom for the rom-com. In hugely successful movies, including *When Harry Met Sally* (1989) and *Sleepless In Seattle* (1993), couples put aside their differences to find love. While most rom-coms still follow the formula, an increasing number challenge it by featuring LGBT characters (*But I'm A Cheerleader*, 1999) or older couples (*The Lovers*, 2017).

RELATED FEATURES
See also
THE COMING OF SOUND
page 22

CARY GRANT
page 76

3-SECOND BIOGRAPHIES
GEORGE CUKOR
1899–1983
Director of many screwball romantic comedies of the 1930s and 1940s, including *The Philadelphia Story*

NORA EPHRON
1941–2012
Writer of modern rom-com classics including *When Harry Met Sally* and *Sleepless in Seattle* (which she also directed)

NANCY MEYERS
1949–
Screenwriter and director of modern rom-coms including *It's Complicated* (2009)

30-SECOND TEXT
Nikki Baughan

It Happened One Night (1934) is an archetypal rom-com, and the genre is still going strong.

SCIENCE FICTION

the 30-second feature

Although its scientists looked more like wizards, its astronauts wore no spacesuits, and its stars, planets and satellites had human faces beaming from their surfaces, Georges Méliès' 1902 silent film *A Trip to the Moon* was probably the first science-fiction film. It also, with its lunar landing and alien encounters, occupied that outer edge of human experience which has come to define the genre. Science fiction is always exploring the frontiers of knowledge, whether matching its narrative trajectories to the speculative itineraries of space and time travel, or testing the sometimes fluid boundaries between humans and technology – like the robot in *Metropolis* (1927), the artificial intelligence in *2001: A Space Odyssey* (1968), and the replicants in *Blade Runner* (1982) – or between humans and aliens (*The Day The Earth Stood Still* and *The Thing From Another World*, both 1951). It can be set in outer or inner space, or in imaginary or multiple universes. The further from Earth it gets, the less science it requires, as the 'space opera' of the *Star Wars* franchise proves. Yet science fiction always merely extrapolates from the ideological realities of the here and now, so that even its most otherworldly or dystopian visions involve reflection on who we are today and where we might be heading.

RELATED FEATURES
See also
EARLY CINEMA
page 16

STEVEN SPIELBERG
page 66

GEORGE LUCAS
page 126

3-SECOND TRAILER
Science fiction tests the outer limits of human knowledge, endeavour and experience, all in the service of exploring who we are.

3-MINUTE SEQUEL
As well as exploring the cutting edge of science, the genre also often utilizes state-of-the-art film-making technologies and special effects. Yet films such as Shane Carruth's time-travelling brain bender *Primer* (2004) and James Ward Byrkit's multiverse puzzler *Coherence* (2013) demonstrate that big ideas do not always require big budgets, while Gareth Edwards' *Monsters* (2010) shows that well-crafted visual razzamatazz can now be achieved on a home computer.

3-SECOND BIOGRAPHIES
PHILIP K. DICK
1928–82
Science-fiction author whose novels have inspired many films including *Blade Runner*, *Total Recall* (1990) and *Minority Report* (2002)

DAVID CRONENBERG
1943–
Writer/director whose films – including *Scanners* (1981), *The Fly* (1986) and *eXistenZ* (1999) – often conjoin body horror with the more cerebral concepts of science fiction

30-SECOND TEXT
Anton Bitel

From Metropolis *to* Star Wars, *science-fiction films explore worlds far beyond our universe, or buried deep in our minds.*

HORROR

the 30-second feature

Typically occupying the ground where monsters stomp, ghosts haunt and mad killers stalk their prey, horror, unlike every other genre, does not derive its name from its content, but rather from the ideal audience response. Horror is a reaction – and whatever inspires dread, unease or abjection is staged by this genre as vicarious entertainment. Horror arrived as early as Georges Méliès' *The Haunted Castle* (1896), found full expression in silent features such as Robert Wiene's *The Cabinet of Dr Caligari* (1920) and F. W. Murnau's influential vampire film *Nosferatu* (1922), and became a recognized genre term with the 'Universal Monsters' of the 1930s and 1940s. In the 1950s, horror films explored anxieties about the Cold War and the atom bomb. In 1968, Roman Polanski's *Rosemary's Baby* and George A. Romero's *Night of the Living Dead* anchored horror to America's domestic uncertainties, ushering in a decade of counter-cultural grit and gore. The slasher (along with extravagant practical special effects) dominated the 1980s. Wes Craven's *New Nightmare* (1994) and *Scream* (1996) featured characters openly aware of their genre and its tropes. Post-millennial horror has been a productive mélange of Japanese technophobia (or 'J-horror'), French extremity, Spanish ghosts, torture porn, found footage and ever-resurgent zombies.

RELATED FEATURES
See also
WES CRAVEN
page 36

ALFRED HITCHCOCK
page 54

GERMAN EXPRESSIONISM
page 94

3-SECOND BIOGRAPHIES
LON CHANEY JR
1906–72
Played all four of Universal Studios' principal monsters in the 1940s: the Wolfman, Frankenstein's Monster, the Mummy and Dracula

GEORGE A. ROMERO
1940–2017
Director renowned for inventing the modern zombie, and for re-energizing the horror genre with sociopolitical and satirical commentary

30-SECOND TEXT
Anton Bitel

3-SECOND TRAILER
Often seen as pandering to its viewers' basest instincts, horror confronts – and entertains – us with the worst of society and human nature.

3-MINUTE SEQUEL
Horror, along with its fan base, frequently provokes suspicion and moral disapproval. It is the genre that falls foul of the censors more than any other. Horror movies are often produced cheaply and independently of the studio system, and viewed through unconventional distribution channels. Despite this existence on the very margins of respectability, there is, paradoxically, no period in film history when horror has not been in demand or profitable.

Killers, zombies, vampires . . . if it scares you, horror films will bring it to life in the dark.

1939
Born in Cleveland, Ohio, USA

1964
Obtains a Master's degree (in philosophy and writing) from Johns Hopkins University

1971
Breaks into editing at a Manhattan film post-production house

1972
Directs his low-budget debut, *The Last House On The Left*

1977
Having failed to get his non-genre screenplays made, Craven reluctantly returns to horror with *The Hills Have Eyes*

1984
Finds new success (and launches a franchise) with *A Nightmare on Elm Street*

1996
Revitalizes the slasher with *Scream*, another franchise-launcher

1999
Finally makes a non-horror film, *Music of the Heart*

2015
Dies of brain cancer at his Los Angeles home

WES CRAVEN

After teaching English and Humanities at various universities on the USA's East Coast, and pseudonymously directing several pornographic films, in 1972 Wes Craven helmed the first feature to bear his own name. *The Last House on the Left* was a reimagining of Ingmar Bergman's rape revenger *The Virgin Spring* (1960), relocated from medieval Sweden to contemporary New York, and capturing the violent polarization of Vietnam-era America. Cheap, scuzzy and uncompromisingly ugly in its portrayal of people from different backgrounds behaving equally badly, this debut established Craven as a horror film-maker very much of the moment. In 1977, *The Hills Have Eyes* again showed a respectable American family summoning its own barely concealed brutality to fight back against a clan of savages.

Craven found originality in old forms with *A Nightmare On Elm Street* (1984), in which a supernatural villain (Robert Englund's Freddy Krueger) stalks and attacks his adolescent victims in their dreams; it revitalized the conventions of the slasher, a sub-genre that was becoming ossified by the mid-1980s. Likewise, if George A. Romero had invented the modern zombie with *Night of the Living Dead* (1968) and its two sequels, influencing countless other film-makers along the way, then Craven predictably went in the opposite direction with his *The Serpent and the Rainbow* (1988), taking the zombie right back to its origins in Haitian folklore and voodoo magic.

Craven's underrated (and hilariously unhinged) *The People Under The Stairs* (1991) transported the dark fairy-tale spirit of *Hansel and Gretel* to a modern Los Angeles ghetto setting, adding sadomasochist fetish gear and a manically gleeful Everett McGill and Wendy Robie (who riffed off the odd couple they had recently played in the TV series *Twin Peaks*). Yet it was in the mid-1990s, when the horror genre seemed to have lost its way, that Craven's love of reinvigorating horror tropes came into its own. His mainstream experiments, *New Nightmare* (1994) and *Scream* (1996), deployed great self-conscious wit to deconstruct respectively his own moribund Elm Street franchise and the slasher sub-genre, setting a tone of self-referential cleverness for the rest of the decade's horror. In 1999 Craven finally got his wish to direct a fright-free drama, *Music from the Heart*, but it is for his contributions to horror that he will always be best known.

Anton Bitel

MUSICALS

the 30-second feature

When sound arrived at the cinema in 1927, a plethora of American musicals followed. Throughout the 1930s, the geometric style of choreographer Busby Berkeley embellished films such as *Gold Diggers of 1933* and *42nd Street*. Meanwhile, Fred Astaire and Ginger Rogers were the epitome of sophistication as they danced across the screen in ten hits, beginning with *Flying Down to Rio* (1933). Songwriting masters including Jerome Kern, George and Ira Gershwin, and Irving Berlin provided the music. The decade finished with the resounding success of MGM's *The Wizard of Oz* (1939). Musicals were reinvigorated in the 1940s with the increased popularity of Technicolor, along with an 'integrated' approach that allowed musical numbers to be incorporated into the narrative. At MGM Studios, producer Arthur Freed formed a legendary in-house group of directors, actors and writers, known as the 'Freed Unit'. Its string of inventive musicals – *Meet Me in St. Louis* (1944), *Singin' in the Rain* (1952), *Gigi* (1958) – made for a 'golden age' of musicals. Despite its permutations, the genre maintained its popularity well into the 1960s as a staple of studio-system Hollywood, with the ever-popular *The Sound of Music* (1965), and theatre mavericks such as Bob Fosse continued to innovate with the form (*Cabaret*, 1972).

3-SECOND TRAILER
Musicals offer boundless spectacle, whether embodying escapism or subversion. While song-and-dance shows may seem lightweight, their impact is born of artistry and professionalism.

3-MINUTE SEQUEL
The screen musical is an enduringly popular form of entertainment around the world. Music and dance have been a vital part of India's Bollywood cinema for the better part of a century. From the early 1930s to contemporary films such as *Devdas* (2002), their colourful and poetic choreography has become world-renowned, and stars including Shah Rukh Khan and Deepika Padukone are beloved for their acting skill as much as for their singing talent.

RELATED FEATURES
See also
THE COMING OF SOUND
page 22

SHAH RUKH KHAN
page 86

THE STUDIO SYSTEM
page 116

3-SECOND BIOGRAPHIES
BUSBY BERKELEY
1895–1976
Golden-Age Hollywood director and choreographer of films including *42nd Street* and *Footlight Parade* (both 1933)

GENE KELLY
1912–96
Singer, dancer and star of *Singin' in the Rain*, *An American in Paris* and others

30-SECOND TEXT
Christina Newland

For many audiences, the song-and-dance magic of musicals offers the ultimate cinematic spectacle.

GANGSTER MOVIES

the 30-second feature

Moral queasiness lingers around the glamour accorded to professional criminals, and the trilbied American mobster was a deeply divisive figure in the initial 1930s' gangster movie boom. Box-office catnip between 1931 and 1934, with over 70 made in a short but influential spree, the gangster film had to fight a running battle with the censors – and ultimately lost. A continuation of American Wild West outlaw worship, the genre rose to popularity on the back of urban audiences in fast-growing cities, titillated by stories of organized-crime kingpins such as Al Capone and Lucky Luciano. Warner Bros was at the forefront of these vicarious and violent pulp stories, releasing both *Little Caesar* and *Public Enemy* in 1931. But it was 1932's *Scarface*, directed by Howard Hawks, which faced the most opprobrium; the director was initially asked to shoot a different ending in which Paul Muni's Capone-inspired hoodlum was hanged. The prevalence of gangster movies perhaps hastened the strict enforcement of the Hays Code in 1934, which defined the moral limits within which Hollywood had to work. The mantle of US crime cinema then passed to the less sensationalizing film noir. The lifting of the Code in 1968 led to a revival of gangster epics under directors such as Francis Ford Coppola, Martin Scorsese and Roman Polanski.

Mobsters are the villains Hollywood can't live without – even if they must pay for their crimes.

DOCUMENTARY
the 30-second feature

The earliest films of ordinary events, such as *The Arrival of a Train at La Ciotat Station* (1896), were in documentary style. With 1922's *Nanook of the North*, the form gained feature-length success and the description 'documentary'. Both observing and staging scenes among Canada's far-north Inuit, Robert Flaherty's pioneering work was typical of the 'exotic' strain that also surfaced in the Soviet Union's parallel documentary boom. The 'city symphony', a poetic montage of urban shots beginning with *Manhatta* (1921), also enjoyed popularity. 1960's *Primary*, following John F. Kennedy and Hubert Humphrey on their election campaign, ushered in a sea change in the ability of documentary film-makers to reflect real life. Lightweight 16mm cameras and improved sound-recording techniques afforded them more intimate contact with their subjects, giving rise to Direct Cinema, named for its authentic dialogue and action; Cinema Vérité, in France, was its sister movement. Later documentary-makers questioned these claims to represent reality so transparently. Yet such aesthetic distinctions seemed secondary during the 2000s commercial revival. Films such as *Bowling for Columbine* (2002) and *Super Size Me* (2004) showed that reality could be as improbable and compelling as anything in a Hollywood blockbuster.

3-SECOND TRAILER
From walrus hunting in the Canadian Arctic to gun culture in Colorado, the documentary examines our world and educates us more directly than any other cinematic genre.

3-MINUTE SEQUEL
Newsreels, invented by Charles Pathé in 1911 and shown in cinemas before the main feature, filled the gap between the early documentary features and the more mobile innovations of the 1960s. Sometimes used for edifying or even nakedly propagandist ends using staged or re-enacted depictions of events, they nonetheless contributed many important films, including Frank Capra's Second World War series *Why We Fight* and the works of Britain's Documentary Film Movement.

RELATED FEATURES
See also
EARLY CINEMA
page 16

SOVIET MONTAGE
page 96

INDEPENDENT CINEMA
page 118

3-SECOND BIOGRAPHIES
ROBERT FLAHERTY
1884–1951
The 'father of documentary' who directed *Nanook of the North*, a dramatic portrayal of the Inuit way of life

MICHAEL MOORE
1954–
Activist and director whose humour and first-person style with *Bowling for Columbine* and *Fahrenheit 9/11* brought the documentary to new heights of commercial success

30-SECOND TEXT
Phil Hoad

From **Nanook of the North** *onwards, documentaries have turned reality into entertainment.*

ANIMATION

the 30-second feature

Not so much a genre in itself as a mode of presentation available to any genre, animation is cinema's most plastic medium, offering film-makers immense freedom to realize their most fanciful visions. The technique goes back to nineteenth-century devices, such as phenakistoscopes and zoetropes, which created the illusion of movement by flicking through a series of minimally different images, and also led to the development of the Cinématographe. Animation comes in many forms: traditional cel animation where each frame is hand-drawn (the Disney classics); stop-motion where puppets (*Anomalisa*, 2015), clay models (*The Curse of the Were-Rabbit*, 2005) or cut-outs (*Fantastic Planet*, 1973) are physically manipulated and photographed frame by frame; rotoscoping, where frames of existing film footage are traced over (*Waking Life*, 2001); and increasingly, computer-generated animation (CGI) – as in Pixar features. While any one of these techniques is often used exclusively in an all-animated film, they can also be combined with each other (Studio Ghibli sometimes mixes cel and CGI), and with live-action footage – for example, 1933's *King Kong*, 1988's *Who Framed Roger Rabbit?* and practically all modern effects-driven blockbusters.

RELATED FEATURES
See also
THE INVENTORS
page 14

DIGITAL FILM-MAKING
page 130

3-SECOND TRAILER
The most flexible and manipulable of film forms, animation brings movement to stills, life to the fanciful and stylization to the real.

3-MINUTE SEQUEL
Animation is, by its nature, a mannered medium, but can now, at least in its high-end computer-generated form, approach a photorealism virtually indistinguishable from live action. Paradoxically, however, the more real it makes its human characters look, the more likely it is to create cognitive dissonance in viewers, alienating them from what they are seeing. This 'uncanny valley' is animation's last frontier.

3-SECOND BIOGRAPHIES
LOTTE REINIGER
1899–1981
An innovator in silhouette animation; her film *The Adventures of Prince Achmed* (1926) is the oldest surviving animated feature

WALT DISNEY
1901–66
Founder of the Walt Disney Company and pioneer in animated feature film-making

HAYAO MIYAZAKI
1941–
Co-founder of Japan's Studio Ghibli, and director of animated features including *Spirited Away* (2001)

30-SECOND TEXT
Anton Bitel

Animation allows film-makers great creative freedom, whether using models, ink or computers.

DIRECTORS

DIRECTORS
GLOSSARY

auteur theory Concept advanced by French film critics in the 1940s, based on the work of André Bazin and Alexandre Astruc and named by US critic Andrew Sarris. While film is a collaborative art, the term 'auteur' is bestowed on directors who impose their own individual vision, style and themes on a film – like the author of a literary work.

axial cut A specific form of jump cut, in which the second camera position is either further from or closer to the object than in the first shot, but along a straight line.

cinécriture Director Agnès Varda's own term for her technique, as 'film-writing', in which a language of moving images, sound and music creates a cohesive whole. The term has many parallels with earlier French critic and director Alexandre Astruc's theory of authorship in film, called the *caméra-stylo*, or 'camera-pen'.

filmography A list of films matching a certain criteria, but most often a list of works by one film-maker.

French New Wave Also known as *La Nouvelle Vague*, this movement in French cinema of the 1950s and 1960s involved a group of young directors including Jean-Luc Godard and François Truffaut. Rejecting literary influences in favour of purely cinematic techniques, and using new lightweight cameras, the New Wave films were youthful, experimental and sometimes political, often using location shooting and authorial commentary. Other New Waves in Britain and Czechoslovakia followed similar principles.

Italian Neorealism Group of films made in post-war Italy by directors including Luchino Visconti, Roberto Rossellini and Vittorio de Sica. Their films featured working-class characters, non-professional actors, location shooting and stories of poverty and oppression in Italian society.

MacGuffin Alfred Hitchcock's term for a plot device that provides narrative momentum but is often revealed to be meaningless – simply an engine to drive the film forward.

New Hollywood Often called the American New Wave, this movement dates roughly from the late 1960s to the early 1980s, and comprises the work of US film-makers influenced by world and arthouse cinema.

Oscar Official nickname for the Academy Awards. The name Oscar was first used in public by Walt Disney in 1932, but there is a dispute over who invented it. Bette Davis claimed in her autobiography that she named the statuette after her first husband, Harmon Oscar Nelson, while others say the Academy's executive secretary Margaret Herrick exclaimed that the figurine looked like her uncle Oscar and the name stuck.

realism This term has two meanings in cinema. Firstly, it is a measure of verisimilitude, or how closely the cinematic image mimics the real world, as in Classical Hollywood cinema. Secondly, it applies to cinema that questions the contrivances that create that illusion: by using only natural light, for example, or by drawing attention to the way that the film is edited.

studio system During the Golden Age of Hollywood, major studios thrived thanks to a combination of factory-inspired production methods, using creative staff on long-term contracts, and vertical integration, that is, the ownership of distribution and exhibition. Anti-trust laws were first used to challenge this monopoly in the late 1940s, leading to the demise of the system by the 1960s.

take A single continuous record of a performance. Directors tend to shoot multiple takes of each scene so that they can choose the best. Long unbroken takes are often used in films as a technique of realism or to build a disquieting sense of tension. Some films appear to have been shot in one single, unedited take, for example, Hitchcock's *Rope* (1948), Andy Warhol's *Empire* (1964), Mike Figgis's *Timecode* (2000) and Sebastian Schipper's *Victoria* (2015).

CHARLIE CHAPLIN
1889–1977

the 30-second feature

'All I need to make a comedy is
a park, a policeman, and a pretty girl.' Charlie
Chaplin's famous description of his early
two-reel comedies is deceptively simplistic.
The slapstick choreography in shorts such as
The Cure or *Easy Street* (both 1917) is as graceful
as it is funny, betraying his patient rehearsal of
gags and his sharp eye for detail. When stage
comic Chaplin first appeared on cinema screens
in 1914 he was an instant, global hit – the biggest
star the medium had yet produced. He began
directing films the same year and by the early
1920s this London lad, who had grown up in
extreme poverty, was a Hollywood heavyweight;
he made feature films such as *The Kid* (1921) and
The Gold Rush (1925), which combined comic
hilarity with poignant sentimentality. Initially
resisting the coming of sound, Chaplin directed
two great near-silent features in the 1930s: *City
Lights* and *Modern Times*. His most audacious
comedy coup was in 1940, when his sound film
The Great Dictator ridiculed Adolf Hitler and
climaxed with a speech condemning fascism.
By 1947, he directed himself against type as a
charming serial killer in the sinister *Monsieur
Verdoux*. He cast himself as a washed-up clown
in the heartbreaking *Limelight* (1952), which
featured a joyous cameo from Chaplin's old
silent comrade in slapstick, Buster Keaton.

RELATED FEATURES
See also
EARLY CINEMA
page 16

SILENT CINEMA
page 18

3-SECOND TRAILER
Chaplin was a star director
who went from slapstick
antics as the 'Little Tramp'
to sophisticated feature
films, and spoofing Hitler.

3-MINUTE SEQUEL
Chaplin appeared in his
famous Little Tramp outfit
of round hat, baggy
trousers and cane in his
first Keystone short films,
directed by others. Although
in those early films he more
often played a working
man than a down-and-out,
this character recurred in
most of Chaplin's films
until the Little Tramp finally
walked into the sunset with
Paulette Goddard at the
end of *Modern Times* (1936).

3-SECOND BIOGRAPHIES
MACK SENNETT
1880–1960
Actor and director specializing
in anarchic slapstick who
founded Keystone Studios in
1912, where many comedians
of the silent era worked

MABEL NORMAND
1892–1930
Actress, screenwriter and
director; the leading female
star at Keystone Studios, she
directed Chaplin and appeared
in 12 films with him

BUSTER KEATON
1895–1966
Comedian, actor and director
famed for his ingenious
physical stunts and deadpan
expression

30-SECOND TEXT
Pamela Hutchinson

*'A park, a policeman
and a pretty girl . . . '
were just the beginning
for Charlie Chaplin.*

STANLEY KUBRICK
1928–1999

the 30-second feature

3-SECOND TRAILER
Stanley Kubrick was a painstaking, perfectionist director – the gaps between his films grew as long as the shadows cast by their Olympian pronouncements on mankind.

3-MINUTE SEQUEL
Known for his exhaustive research as well as for asking actors for numerous takes, Kubrick had to leave the USA to safeguard his level of fastidiousness. Based in the UK from 1961, he enjoyed almost complete autonomy from Hollywood studios, while being largely funded by Warner Bros. He adapted his shooting conditions to these circumstances, most famously filming the Vietnam-set *Full Metal Jacket* (1987) in London, Cambridgeshire and Norfolk.

A reputedly reclusive director, who later exercised total creative control over his work, Stanley Kubrick spelled out his view of human nature in a 13-film oeuvre that is as striking for its pessimism as for its dazzling, imperious style. The title of his experimental debut, *Fear and Desire* (1953), sums up the existential drives ruling his often pawn-like protagonists. These figures are at the mercy of a godless universe, or one ruled by a directorial deity bent on satirizing the human condition. This was the Kubrick who adapted Nabokov's 'unfilmable' *Lolita* (1962) and made black comedy from nuclear annihilation in *Dr Strangelove* (1964). His *2001: A Space Odyssey* (1968), was a great leap forward for science-fiction cinema and a psychedelic touchstone for David Bowie, among others. He continued to innovate, using NASA-developed lenses to shoot literary adaptation *Barry Lyndon* (1975) by candlelight, and employing long Steadicam takes to give *The Shining* (1980) its lingering air of intimidation. But viewing humanity through a long lens never crushed his satirical bent, or his obligation to his fallible characters. This duality peaks in his most controversial film, 1971's *A Clockwork Orange*, subsequently withdrawn in Britain by the director himself. He disapproved of 'ultraviolent' thug Alex, but also of the system that demands his reform at the expense of human free will.

RELATED FEATURES
See also
SCIENCE FICTION
page 32

STEVEN SPIELBERG
page 66

THE STUDIO SYSTEM
page 116

3-SECOND BIOGRAPHIES
JOHN ALCOTT
1931–86
Cinematographer; Kubrick's key collaborator through his imperial phase from *2001: A Space Odyssey* to *The Shining*

JAN HARLAN
1937–
Executive producer; long-time collaborator and brother-in-law of Christiane Kubrick, the director's third wife; the pair now manage the director's extensive archives

30-SECOND TEXT
Phil Hoad

The ultimate perfectionist, Stanley Kubrick created classics including A Clockwork Orange, The Shining *and* Dr Strangelove.

1899
Born in Leytonstone, England

1920
Works full-time at Islington Studios, London

1926
Marries screenwriter Alma Reville, who becomes his lifelong collaborator

1927
Makes his first thriller, *The Lodger: A Story of the London Fog*

1939
Leaves England for Hollywood. *Rebecca* (1940), his first film made there, wins an Oscar award for Best Picture

1943
Shadow of a Doubt is released, Hitchcock's favourite of all his films

1945
Hitchcock's first Technicolor film, *Rope*

1958
The now critically acclaimed *Vertigo* performs poorly at the box office

1960
Film critic of the British newspaper *The Observer*, C. A. Lejeune, is so badly offended by *Psycho* that she retires

1979
Receives knighthood, rather belatedly

1980
Dies of renal failure in his home in Bel Air, Los Angeles, USA

ALFRED HITCHCOCK

Born at the turn of the nineteenth century, Alfred Hitchcock would define the cinema of the twentieth. From his first thriller, the silent *The Lodger: A Story of the London Fog* (1927), he regularly gave himself background walk-on roles in his films. These cameos were essential to the branding of a director who would also appear frequently in interviews and trailers, and eventually host *Alfred Hitchcock Presents* on television (1955–65).

Hitchcock honed his skills in creating thrillers coloured by macabre humour with a series of films, including *The 39 Steps* (1935) and *The Lady Vanishes* (1938), which saw him feted as Britain's best director of the time. In 1939, he headed to Hollywood where he earned the title 'master of suspense'. Hitchcock developed the MacGuffin, an arbitrary plot-motivating device. He also exhibited a predilection for wrongly accused men, dominating mothers, platinum blondes (typically Grace Kelly, Janet Leigh or Tippi Hedren), fugitives and sociopathic killers, and liked to set their struggles against real landmarks: the dome of the British Museum in *Blackmail* (1929), the Royal Albert Hall in *The Man Who Knew Too Much* (both 1934 and 1956) and the Statue of Liberty in *Saboteur* (1942).

He was a director who was always innovating. *Blackmail* (1929) was Britain's first full talkie, while *Dial M For Murder* (1954) experimented with 3D. Hitchcock confined the events of *Lifeboat* (1944) to a single, small rescue vessel, of *Rope* (1948) to an apartment and an apparent – if not actual – single shot, and of *Rear Window* (1954) once again to a single apartment and the voyeuristic (yet trapped) perspective of its wheelchair-using hero (James Stewart). He constantly pushed at the limits of what was acceptable in cinema, perhaps most famously in the proto-slasher *Psycho* (1960). The shockingly violent shower murder sequence was immediately preceded by mainstream cinema's first on-screen flushing toilet – a sure sign that the conventions of contemporary morality were about to be sent down the drain.

Psycho, along with Hitchcock's other masterworks *Vertigo* (1958) and *The Birds* (1963), illustrated the director's preoccupation with Freudian psychology, as did *Spellbound* (1945), with its elaborate dream sequences designed by Salvador Dalí. *Vertigo*, a complex story of obsession and duplicity, introduced the dolly zoom, and was voted the greatest film of all time in *Sight & Sound's* 2012 critics' poll.

Anton Bitel

SATYAJIT RAY
1921–1992

the 30-second feature

The steam train that exhilarates

the rural children in Satyajit Ray's 1955 debut *Pather Panchali* was a symbol of the progress he believed was necessary for newly independent India, and also of his own smooth track past his country's cinematic traditions. Ray had assisted Jean Renoir on his 1951 film *The River* and was greatly influenced by the Frenchman's poetic realism. Rejecting the florid, musical style popular in Indian commercial cinema in favour of this steady, westernized focus, he chronicled the coming of age of a Bengali village boy in his moving, sensitively filmed Apu Trilogy. His Parallel Cinema movement ran alongside India's populist film-production hubs, and initially found more acclaim on the arthouse and festival circuit abroad than at home. Yet although his lucid realism distanced him from most other Indian directors, he paradoxically produced works that represented his country in exquisite microcosm. 1964's *Charulata* ('The Lonely Wife'), regarded as his masterpiece, takes place almost entirely inside a bourgeois Calcutta house, a gilded cage for a bored spouse. Ray later engaged more deeply with social issues in his 1970s Calcutta Trilogy. Dependent on government patronage, Parallel Cinema fizzled out in the 1990s, but Ray's reputation as one of cinema's great humanists had already transcended it.

3-SECOND TRAILER
Satyajit Ray turned away from Bollywood escapism and became a world-cinema master to stand with Jean Renoir, Yasujiro Ozu and Ingmar Bergman.

3-MINUTE SEQUEL
All but two of Ray's 36 films were in the minority Bengali language, not Hindi – a sign of the director's fidelity to grassroots realities, despite the foreign influence on his film-making methods and style. He briefly flirted with Hollywood in 1969 when he went to Los Angeles to sell his script for *The Alien*; it was never made, but has often been cited as an influence on Steven Spielberg's *E.T.* (1982).

RELATED FEATURES
See also
SHAH RUKH KHAN
page 86

ITALIAN NEOREALISM
page 102

ARTHOUSE CINEMA
page 138

3-SECOND BIOGRAPHIES
JEAN RENOIR
1894–1979
Director and Ray's mentor during the long development of *Pather Panchali*

RITWIK GHATAK
1925–76
Fellow Parallel Cinema director who made his own, mythology-infused Calcutta Trilogy

SOUMITRA CHATTERJEE
1935–
Actor; starred in 15 of Ray's films, including *Charulata*, and two as Feluda, the 'Bengali Sherlock Holmes'

30-SECOND TEXT
Phil Hoad

Satyajit Ray is now celebrated widely as one of cinema's great humanists.

INGMAR BERGMAN
1918–2007

the 30-second feature

3-SECOND TRAILER
Swedish auteur who made
some of cinema's greatest
masterpieces and explored
timeless themes including
faith and mortality.

3-MINUTE SEQUEL
Bergman often worked
with the same cast and
crew, among them Swedish
cinematographer Sven
Nykvist, who won two
Academy Awards for his
work on *Cries and Whispers*
and *Fanny and Alexander*.
Much more controversial
were Bergman's romantic
affairs with the recurring
stars of his films, actresses
Bibi Andersson, Harriet
Andersson and Liv Ullmann.
His reputation as a
possessive director and the
preoccupation with female
sexuality in his films
frequently complicate
feminist readings of them.

Ingmar Bergman remains one of
the world's most beloved filmmakers thanks to
a prolific oeuvre that includes some of the most
influential films of all time. He began his career
in the 1940s as a screenwriter in his native Sweden.
Smiles of a Summer Night (1955) earned him his
first taste of international acclaim, which he
followed with the renowned medieval epic *The
Seventh Seal* (1957), in which a knight played by
Max von Sydow plays chess with Death, and
Wild Strawberries (1957), starring silent-era
Swedish director Victor Sjostrom as an ageing
professor looking back on his youth. Throughout
his sprawling career, Bergman would frequently
challenge classic themes such as religion, family
and marriage, and many of his films centralized
a female perspective. The women in Bergman
films often grapple with questions of sexuality
in conservative societies, perhaps most famously
in *Persona* (1966), which explores the tenuous
relationship between a young nurse and her
actress patient. *Persona* is widely considered to
be Bergman's masterpiece, but his films *Cries
and Whispers* (1972) and *Fanny and Alexander*
(1982) have been deemed just as critical to the
power of his legacy and his exploration of
human nature. He also produced more than 170
plays and made fruitful ventures into television,
most notably with *Scenes from a Marriage* (1973).

RELATED FEATURES
See also
INDEPENDENT CINEMA
page 118

ARTHOUSE CINEMA
page 138

3-SECOND BIOGRAPHY
LIV ULLMANN
1938–
Norwegian actress and director
who starred in many of
Bergman's films and directed
Faithless (2000)

30-SECOND TEXT
Kelli Weston

*Prolific and provocative,
Bergman is renowned
for a vast oeuvre
including the fêted
classics* **Persona** *and*
The Seventh Seal.

AGNÈS VARDA
1928–

the 30-second feature

Belgian-born French director

Agnès Varda is one of the defining figures of the French New Wave, which critics have characterized as a break with conventional techniques and narratives in favour of visually experimental films layered with social commentary. Varda began her career as a photographer, and although her films boast a documentary-style realism, she drew inspiration from the surrealists. She practised what she called *cinécriture* (cinema writing), her unique style of film-making, and made an assured directorial debut at 25 with the film *La Pointe Courte* (1955), about a couple struggling through their rocky marriage. Varda frequently engages with feminist themes in her films, centralizing the female voice and perspective. *Cléo de 5 à 7* (1961) follows a young singer for two hours while she awaits the results of a biopsy. Meanwhile *Le Bonheur* (1965) tells the story of a happily married man who embarks on an affair, and the two women at the mercy of his desires. She also tackled race in her 1968 short documentary *Black Panthers*. Her husband, fellow New Wave director Jacques Demy, had a great influence on her work and inspired her films *Jacquot de Nantes* (1991) and *The World of Jacques Demy* (1995).

3-SECOND TRAILER
Agnès Varda rose to prominence with the French New Wave and remains one of cinema's most influential directors.

3-MINUTE SEQUEL
Varda describes *cinécriture* as an intricate and elaborate combination of moving images, sound and music. 'Cinema writing' is distinct from screenwriting for Varda, who believes *cinécriture* to be the meticulous effort of film-making – everything from the choice of lighting to the editing of music – and the sensations that endeavour creates for audiences. Varda explains: 'You know, it's a handmade work of film-making – that I really believe. And I call that cine-writing.'

RELATED FEATURES
See also
ITALIAN NEOREALISM
page 102

FRENCH NEW WAVE
page 106

FEMINIST CINEMA
page 140

3-SECOND BIOGRAPHY
JACQUES DEMY
1931–90
French director and screenwriter, best known for his distinct visuals and 1964 musical *Les Parapluies de Cherbourg* (*The Umbrellas of Cherbourg*)

30-SECOND TEXT
Kelli Weston

Agnès Varda described the way sound, image, editing and lighting all come together in her distinctive film-making as cinécriture.

ANDRZEJ WAJDA
1926–2016

the 30-second feature

Director Andrzej Wajda found
international acclaim with stirring cinematic
portraits of his native Poland, unravelling its
history and complex cultural identity. Wajda
came of age as the Second World War ravaged
Europe; Poland endured five years of German
occupation, and Wajda's films would examine
the consequences of this trauma on his country.
In the wake of tragedies both personal and
political, the director crafted the war trilogy he
would later become best remembered for: *A
Generation* (1954), *Kanal* (1956) and *Ashes and
Diamonds* (1958). Throughout his filmography,
Wajda grappled with the political and collective
psychological effects of war and oppressive
regimes on Poland, not just explicitly, but
allegorically, in films such as *Lotna* (1959) and
Siberian Lady Macbeth (1962). Over the next
two decades of his career, Wajda battled
Communist censorship in his home country as
he continued to make blatantly political films,
including *Man of Iron* (1981) – his follow-up to
Man of Marble (1976) – which follows the Polish
Solidarity labour movement. Throughout the
1970s and 1980s, he produced work abroad,
primarily in Germany and France, such as *A Love
in Germany* (1983), and also worked extensively
in the theatre before his death in 2016.

3-SECOND TRAILER
A formidable presence
in European cinema,
Andrzej Wajda made films
dedicated to exploring
quintessentially Polish
culture and history.

3-MINUTE SEQUEL
Wajda belonged to what
was informally known as
the 'Polish Film School',
a close circle of Polish
film-makers – graduates of
Łódź Film School – whose
films reflected the political
and social climate of
Poland in the aftermath of
the Second World War. The
Polish Film School, like the
French New Wave, was
heavily influenced by
Italian Neorealism. Its
members were active
throughout the mid-1950s
and early 1960s, and
regularly worked together.

RELATED FEATURES
See also
ITALIAN NEOREALISM
page 102

FRENCH NEW WAVE
page 106

CULT CINEMA
page 150

3-SECOND BIOGRAPHIES
ANDRZEJ MUNK
1921–1961
One of Poland's most
renowned film-makers, who
directed many classics of Polish
cinema such as *Man on the
Tracks* (1956)

ROMAN POLANSKI
1933–
Internationally recognized,
controversial Polish film-maker,
director of classics such as
Knife in the Water (1962) and
Rosemary's Baby (1968)

30-SECOND TEXT
Kelli Weston

*Andrzej Wajda's films
brought the complex
history and trauma
of his native Poland
to the screen.*

PEDRO ALMODÓVAR
1949–

the 30-second feature

Spanish film-maker Pedro

Almodóvar's oeuvre is eclectic, but lovable characters at the margins of society may well be his career's defining thread. In the wake of Francisco Franco's death in 1975, Almodóvar became a leading figure of the *La Movida Madrileña* (the Madrid Scene), a hedonistic and artistic socio-cultural movement. His early films celebrated the political and, in particular, the sexual freedom of Spain's post-dictatorship years. Almodóvar's feature-length debut *Pepi, Luci, Bom* (1980), a feminist comedy about the unlikely friendship forged between three women – a rape survivor, a masochistic housewife and a lesbian punk-rock singer – set the stage for themes the prolific director would explore with humour and depth throughout his career. Comedy often underpins darker elements such as sexual transgression and dysfunctional families; likewise, womanhood and female relationships are prevalent in his filmography. *Woman on the Verge of a Nervous Breakdown* (1988) earned him international acclaim. Mother-daughter relationships in conflict drive the drama in films such as *High Heels* (1991), *Volver* (2006) and *Julieta* (2016). Recognized as a pioneering figure in queer cinema, Almodóvar frequently incorporates LGBTQ experiences and perspectives into his films.

RELATED FEATURES
See also
FEMINIST FILM-MAKING
page 140

NEW QUEER CINEMA
page 142

3-SECOND BIOGRAPHY
LUIS BUÑUEL
1900–83
Spanish film-maker, a pioneer of surrealist film, and considered one of cinema's most influential directors

30-SECOND TEXT
Kelli Weston

3-SECOND TRAILER
Pedro Almodóvar has won widespread acclaim and a cult following with narratives that centralize the marginalized and explore family, identity and sexuality.

3-MINUTE SEQUEL
Almodóvar repeatedly works with the same performers: Penélope Cruz, Rossy de Palma, Cecilia Roth and Antonio Banderas, all high-profile Spanish actors, some of whom owe their initial success to Almodóvar. The Spanish actresses who frequently appear in the director's films have been dubbed *chicas Almodóvar* – 'Almodóvar's women'. The director considers his films 'very Spanish' and most have been shot in Spain.

Pedro Almodóvar's eclectic oeuvre frequently features lovable but marginalized figures.

STEVEN SPIELBERG
1946–

the 30-second feature

A child of the 1970s New

Hollywood movement that shook up the studio system, Steven Spielberg also spelled its end. When *Jaws*, his third feature, opened in 1975 and was the first film to earn $100 million at the box office, it ushered in the modern blockbuster era. Spielberg also set the style for a new decade of entertainment – breathless, awestruck and studded with quips. His own early trio of hits, *Close Encounters of the Third Kind* (1977), *Raiders of the Lost Ark* (1981) and *E.T.* (1982), set the bar – and displayed a signature childlike exhilaration that lifted his work beyond mere precocious action sequences. As he became a lynchpin of modern Hollywood, founding his own studio, Dreamworks, in 1994, Spielberg extended his range beyond popcorn entertainment into lofty humanism. He won best director and best picture awards for 1993's *Schindler's List*; the same year he reclaimed the accolade for the highest grossing film ever with *Jurassic Park*. No other director has straddled the twin worlds of the multiplex and the prestige picture with such self-assurance. Though his more recent films have not been the singular events of old, Spielbergian sensibility still thrums in the cultural backdrop, clearly visible in the work of director J. J. Abrams and US TV series *Stranger Things*.

3-SECOND TRAILER
The wunderkind director who showed 1970s Hollywood it was time for 'a bigger boat', changing its course from auteur visions towards big box-office bucks.

3-MINUTE SEQUEL
The combined US box-office gross of Spielberg's films was around $4.5 billion in 2017, making him the most financially successful director to date. He most effectively combined the often competing demands of multiplex and arthouse in 1998's *Saving Private Ryan*; the 27-minute opening sequence depicting the assault on Omaha beach once again showed his mastery of action film-making. The movie grossed nearly $500m worldwide and won five Oscars.

RELATED FEATURES
See also
NEW HOLLYWOOD
page 108

THE STUDIO SYSTEM
page 116

GEORGE LUCAS
page 126

3-SECOND BIOGRAPHIES
SID SHEINBERG
1935–
President of Universal Pictures, protected the young director during Jaws' problematic shoot and formed a 20-year working relationship with him.

KATHLEEN KENNEDY
1953–
Producer and co-founder of Spielberg's first production company Amblin Entertainment

30-SECOND TEXT
Phil Hoad

*Blockbuster auteur Steven Spielberg created hugely successful action movies such as **Jaws** and the Indiana Jones films.*

ABBAS KIAROSTAMI
1940–2016

the 30-second feature

The leading figure of the Iranian New Wave that began in the late 1960s before the revolution, Abbas Kiarostami proved that it was possible to create high art under a repressive Islamic regime. Also a painter, illustrator, graphic designer and advertising director, he rose to international acclaim as part of the New Wave's second phase in the 1980s. His Koker trilogy, beginning with *Where Is The Friend's Home?* (1987) imbued mundane events in a northern Iranian village with the weight of timeless parables, recalling Italian Neorealism. But Kiarostami revitalized cinema further. The third in the trilogy, 1994's *Through the Olive Trees*, featured Kiarostami's own crew making a second film in the earthquake-hit village. Possibly inspired by the French New Wave, these self-referential games weren't used in the Western postmodern way to make ironic sport with the form. Rather, blending fiction and documentary, they evolved into tender probings of the interplay between life and art in works that cemented Kiarostami's world-auteur status. His 1990 film *Close-Up* centred on a conman impersonating his fellow New-Wave artist Mohsen Makhmalbaf; 1997's *Taste of Cherry*, which follows a middle-aged man as he plans suicide, was driven by the sense of earnest moral inquiry that still motivates the likes of film-maker Asghar Farhadi today.

RELATED FEATURES
See also
ITALIAN NEOREALISM
page 102

FESTIVALS
page 120

ARTHOUSE CINEMA
page 138

3-SECOND TRAILER
Abbas Kiarostami was a tireless interlocutor with cinema and life, who brought Iranian film to the world's attention.

3-MINUTE SEQUEL
Making children's films was one way to avoid the censors in post-revolution Iran. Like several of his peers, Kiarostami began his directorial career making short films at Kunan, the Institute for the Intellectual Development of Children and Young Adults. The oil money that helped fund this public body was at least partly responsible for Iran's cinematic boom under the ayatollahs, increasing from 28 films in 1980 to 87 by 2001.

3-SECOND BIOGRAPHIES
DARIUSH MEHRJUI
1939–
Director of *The Cow* (1969), reportedly admired by Ayatollah Khomeini, and considered the first Iranian New-Wave film

MOHSEN MAKHMALBAF
1957–
Former anti-royalist militant turned director of more than 20 films; his daughters Samira and Hana are also directors

30-SECOND TEXT
Phil Hoad

Abbas Kiarostami's timeless films, including **Close-Up** *and* **Taste of Cherry,** *proved that it was possible to make great art even under an oppressive regime.*

STARS ◑

Bollywood Informal term for the Hindi-language film industry in India, based in Mumbai, formerly known as Bombay (hence the B in Bollywood). Just as not all American films are made in Hollywood, not all Indian films are made in Bollywood. It is, however, the largest film producer in India, which makes more movies per year than any other country. While Bollywood was known for socially aware realist films in the 1940s and 1950s, since the 1970s it has become largely identified with lavish musical romances and action thrillers.

method acting Russian actor and director Konstantin Stanislavski developed this influential approach to performance in the early twentieth century, and it was further popularized by Lee Strasberg and his colleagues at the Actors Studio in New York in the 1950s. Often described as an actor's total immersion in a character, method acting is a way for a performer to find a deep emotional identification with a particular role. Marlon Brando, Marilyn Monroe and Dustin Hoffman are famous cinema method actors.

New Hollywood Often called the American New Wave, this movement dates roughly from the late 1960s to the early 1980s, and comprises the work of US film-makers influenced by world and arthouse cinema.

Oscar Official nickname for the Academy Awards. The name Oscar was first used in public by Walt Disney in 1932, but there is a dispute over who invented it. Bette Davis claimed in her autobiography that she named the statuette after her first husband, Harmon Oscar Nelson, while others say the Academy's executive secretary Margaret Herrick exclaimed that the figurine looked like her uncle Oscar and the name stuck.

rom-com Popular abbreviation for romantic comedy, which has shifted to mean specifically a light, female-oriented film, often denigrated as formulaic. Conversely, romantic comedies directed by male auteurs transcend the label.

talkie Colloquial term for a sound film: after silent 'movies' came the sound 'talkies'. However, the term 'movies' remains in use for all films, while 'talkie' is used only to describe early sound films.

yakuza An operative of an organized crime syndicate in Japan. *Yakuza* have been popular figures in Japanese national cinema since the silent era. *Yakuza* films often betray the influence of classic Hollywood gangster films, but some, such as the 'existential' *yakuza* films directed by Takeshi Kitano, offer a new slant on this violent movie genre.

MARY PICKFORD
1892–1979

the 30-second feature

3-SECOND TRAILER
Beautiful, ringletted star who played young girls on-screen but was a formidable, painstaking producer off-screen, with complete creative control over her later work.

3-MINUTE SEQUEL
'I would like to concentrate on acting alone', Pickford said, 'but I realize I can't. I must be responsible for the entire production. So many things can ruin fine work.' Her star-producer model was popular with her contemporaries, including Gloria Swanson and Norma Talmadge. Although the studio system limited the independence of stars, recent actresses to emulate this model include Jodie Foster, Drew Barrymore, Angelina Jolie and Reese Witherspoon.

Known to the public as 'America's sweetheart', behind the scenes Mary Pickford was also a producer, who had creative control over her films and was a co-founder of United Artists in 1919. Aged 15, Gladys Smith from Toronto got her big break, and her stage name, on Broadway and in 1909 talked her way into a job at D. W. Griffith's Biograph Company in New York for $40 a week. After years of making films for others at a prolific rate, in 1916 she signed a contract with Famous Players-Lasky that gave her full creative authority. Both there and later at United Artists, Pickford carefully nurtured her persona, starring in hit silent movies including 1926's Expressionist-style tearjerker *Sparrows* and romantic comedy *My Best Girl* (1927). She often played much younger, very spirited women and children in these films, many of which were written by Frances Marion. Her devoted fans coped with the scandal of her early divorce and remarriage to Douglas Fairbanks in 1919, but had to steel themselves for another shock with her decision to bob her ringlets and play a socialite in 1929's Oscar-winning talkie *The Coquette*. She continued to work as a producer after her last screen role in 1934.

RELATED FEATURES
See also
EARLY CINEMA
page 16

SILENT CINEMA
page 18

D. W. GRIFFITH
page 20

3-SECOND BIOGRAPHIES
DOUGLAS FAIRBANKS
1883–1939
Acrobatic, swashbuckling, occasionally self-mocking Hollywood star; married to Mary Pickford 1920–36, during which time they became Hollywood royalty

FRANCES MARION
1888–1973
Oscar-winning screenwriter and producer who had a fruitful collaboration with Pickford in the 1920s, and wrote many defining films of the era

30-SECOND TEXT
Pamela Hutchinson

A powerhouse both in front of and behind the camera, Mary Pickford was an early, and very successful, star-producer.

CARY GRANT
1904–1986

the 30-second feature

A rare combination of romantic lead and knockabout comic, Cary Grant is still the byword for Hollywood sophistication and charm. As he once quipped: 'Everybody wants to be Cary Grant. Even I want to be Cary Grant.' He started out playing opposite Mae West and Marlene Dietrich in the early 1930s, but found his niche in the late 1930s and 1940s in screwball comedies and romantic dramas. Born in Bristol, England as Archibald Leach, he originally worked in a travelling circus as an acrobat, and would later put that athleticism to use in his pratfalling physical comedy. In classic screwballs including *Bringing Up Baby* (1938) and *His Girl Friday* (1941) he was as much the handsome leading man as he was the slapstick clown, wrapping his clipped mid-Atlantic accent around the snappy dialogue. Grant mastered more serious roles too. In Howard Hawks' *Only Angels Have Wings* (1939) and Alfred Hitchcock's *Notorious* (1946), his smouldering charisma lent itself to playing self-contained charmers that women could never quite figure out. He would go on to star in some of Hitchcock's most glamorous mid-century films: *To Catch a Thief* (1955) and *North by Northwest* (1959). Before retiring, he appeared with Audrey Hepburn, a star from the younger generation, in *Charade* (1963), which neatly combined his preferred genres of rom-com and thriller.

3-SECOND TRAILER
Cary Grant's winning combination of romantic charm and comic timing made him an unusually versatile leading man, as his string of Hollywood classics attest.

3-MINUTE SEQUEL
For a fantastic summary and examination of Grant's career, try New York film critic Pauline Kael's 1975 essay 'The Man From Dream City'. She examines the vagaries of Grant's stardom and his strong romantic appeal to female viewers, and elegantly analyses his individual film roles. Kael was a hugely influential film critic, and her work on Grant is among her finest writing.

RELATED FEATURES
See also
ROM-COM
page 30

ALFRED HITCHCOCK
page 54

THE STUDIO SYSTEM
page 116

3-SECOND BIOGRAPHY
KATHARINE HEPBURN
1907–2003
American actress who starred with Grant in comedies such as *Bringing Up Baby* and *The Philadelphia Story* (1940)

30-SECOND TEXT
Christina Newland

Excelling at comedy, romance and thrillers, Cary Grant was an all-round star. Hitchcock's North by Northwest *showcases all his skills.*

1901
Born in Berlin, Germany

1922
Makes her silent-film debut

1930
Stars in *The Blue Angel*, Germany's first talkie, and becomes an international star

1931
Signs a contract with Paramount Studios in Hollywood and continues to make films with director Josef von Sternberg

1934
The Shanghai Express is released

1934–39
Ends partnership with Sternberg and is dubbed 'box office poison' until she stars opposite James Stewart in popular western *Destry Rides Again* (1939)

1945
Awarded the Presidential Medal of Freedom for services to the Allied troops during the Second World War

1948–61
Stars for a series of Hollywood studio directors, including Alfred Hitchcock, Billy Wilder and Orson Welles; she also begins a thriving singing career

1992
Dies aged 91 in her home in Paris, France

MARLENE DIETRICH

Powerful, glamorous and a

proto-feminist icon of Hollywood stardom, Marlene Dietrich seemed to be born for the spotlight. Beginning her career as a chorus girl and then a silent-screen star in her native Berlin, Germany, Dietrich had her break-out role as a nightclub chanteuse in *The Blue Angel* (1930). Germany's first talkie was a hit, partly due to Dietrich's commanding voice in her classic song *Falling in Love Again*. The film was directed by her long-time collaborator Josef von Sternberg, and together the pair worked to create a glamorous star persona and flawless image, via costume, cosmetics and lighting. Dietrich was carefully made up to give an otherworldly, sharp-featured appearance – thinly plucked brows, contoured cheekbones, peroxide-blonde hair and a halo of overhead lighting. Sternberg invented this so-called 'butterfly lighting' specifically for Dietrich.

After both director and star moved to Hollywood, Dietrich's exotic look seduced American audiences, who flocked to her films in the first half of the 1930s. Together, she and Sternberg made seven films, among them Dietrich's most famous: *Morocco (1930)*, *The Shanghai Express* (1932) and *Blonde Venus (1932)*. In these films, Dietrich is a powerful seductive force, subverting gender in masculine clothes but always transmitting a powerful, feminine sexuality. In *Morocco* risqué Dietrich dresses in a tuxedo and kisses a woman during a stage routine. Coming of age in the gay clubs of louche Weimar Berlin, Dietrich was more comfortable with her bisexuality than most women of the time, and she has been an LGBTQ icon ever since.

During the Second World War, the German emigré worked hard to support the Allied war effort. She rejected Nazi entreaties to return to the German film industry, became a US citizen in 1939, and worked tirelessly to raise war bonds and entertain American troops; she also recorded anti-Nazi records. By the end of the war, she was awarded a Presidential Medal of Freedom for her contribution.

After the war, Dietrich starred in several films for Billy Wilder – *A Foreign Affair* (1948) and *Witness for the Prosecution* (1957) – but failed to win an Academy Award for these impressive dramatic performances. Perhaps her most memorable late role was in Orson Welles' *Touch of Evil* (1958) as a shrewd fortune-teller. Her immortal line in that film sums up a career of defiant nonconformity, 'What does it matter what you say about people?'

Christina Newland

TOSHIRO MIFUNE
1920–1997

the 30-second feature

'This baby. It's me. It's what happened to me!' says Kikuchiyo (Toshiro Mifune) in Akiro Kurosawa's *Seven Samurai* (1954), as he realizes he has helped create an orphan. With his false name, invented samurai status and animalistic swagger, Kikuchiyo is the one misfit in this otherwise coherent group of nobles, reflecting the actor's own outsider experience growing up in China and Manchuria. Yet thanks to Mifune's gruffly charismatic and earthy humanity, Kikuchiyo is the character with whom viewers most readily identify (much as Kikuchiyo identifies with the baby). Mifune starred in 16 of Kurosawa's films at the peak of the director's career, making him the most popular Japanese actor of his generation. In their earliest collaboration *Drunken Angel* (1948), Mifune offered cinema's first portrayal of a post-war *yakuza*, and in *Seven Samurai*, *Yojimbo* (1961) and *Sanjuro* (1962) he created the archetypal 'wandering warrior with no name' who would be appropriated in many spaghetti westerns. Mifune appeared in over 150 features by other directors, including Kenji Mizoguchi's *The Life of Oharu* (1952), John Boorman's *Hell in the Pacific* (1968) and Jerry London's mini-series *Shogun* (1980). Although he and Kurosawa fell out over the prolonged shoot of *Red Beard* (1965), their best work was done together.

3-SECOND TRAILER
A frequent collaborator with Akira Kurosawa and an imposing, mercurial presence, Toshiro Mifune was the finest Japanese actor of his generation.

3-MINUTE SEQUEL
Though best known for his surly presence and electrifying on-screen emotional displays, Mifune also had impressive range. Aged only 35, he convincingly played an elderly patriarch in Kurosawa's *I Live In Fear* (1955). With even more extreme improbability, in Ismael Rodríguez's *Ánimas Trujano* (1962) he took the lead role as a native Mexican, studying tapes of Mexican actors speaking to ensure that he would be in sync for the Spanish dubbing artist.

RELATED FEATURE
See also
JAPAN'S GOLDEN AGE
page 104

3-SECOND BIOGRAPHIES
AKIRA KUROSAWA
1910–88
Director of *Seven Samurai* and 15 other films in which Mifune starred

SETSUKO HARA
1920–2015
Actress; Mifune's co-star in Akira Kurosawa's *The Idiot* (1951), best known for her collaborations with master director Yasujiro Ozu

30-SECOND TEXT
Anton Bitel

Toshiro Mifune is best known for his collaborations with Akira Kurosawa, including the classic Seven Samurai.

MARILYN MONROE
1926–1962

the 30-second feature

Born Norma Jean Baker in 1926, Marilyn Monroe was destined to become a worldwide cultural icon. With her platinum-blonde locks and hourglass figure, she was both celebrated for her bombshell beauty and hamstrung by it. Starting off as a risqué pin-up model, Marilyn got her first major role in 1950 in John Huston's *The Asphalt Jungle*. Soon her persona as a sex symbol was solidified, and by 1953's *Niagara*, she was one of 20th Century Fox's most bankable stars. Famous for her breathy baby voice and 'dumb blonde' antics, Marilyn starred in a series of frothy commercial comedies and hits. She was a gifted comedienne with an excellent sense of timing and lightning-bolt charisma, perhaps best used in Billy Wilder's cross-dressing comedy *Some Like it Hot* (1959). Marilyn studied at the Actors Studio, in the hope of transcending the ditzy Hollywood typecasting that plagued her for much of her career. Sadly, she struggled to find many challenging roles and rarely played against type. Two broken marriages, drug and alcohol dependency, and depression left her in a fragile state of mind. Under still-debated circumstances, Marilyn was found dead of a barbiturate overdose in 1962, aged only 36.

3-SECOND TRAILER
Iconic, tragic blonde Marilyn Monroe was an often underestimated actress and musical performer of dazzling quality, with an unusually innocent sex appeal.

3-MINUTE SEQUEL
From singing 'Diamonds Are a Girl's Best Friend' to the famous sleeper-train scene in *Some Like it Hot*, Monroe was spellbinding on the screen. She has become a cultural icon, but also a cautionary tale about the treatment of women in Hollywood. To see her in a rare departure from her lighthearted roles, watch her final film, John Huston's *The Misfits*, a desperately sad portrayal of a neurotic divorcee.

RELATED FEATURES
See also
ROM-COMS
page 30

MUSICALS
page 38

THE STUDIO SYSTEM
page 116

3-SECOND BIOGRAPHIES
HOWARD HAWKS
1896–1977
Hollywood studio director of Monroe comedies *Monkey Business* (1952) and *Gentlemen Prefer Blondes* (1953)

BILLY WILDER
1906–2002
German emigré director of two of Monroe's most iconic films: *The Seven Year Itch* (1955) and *Some Like it Hot*

30-SECOND TEXT
Christina Newland

Legendary star Marilyn Monroe died young, leaving behind a string of show-stopping film performances.

ROBERT DE NIRO
1943–

the 30-second feature

When Robert De Niro played the young Vito Corleone, the role made iconic by Marlon Brando, in 1974's *The Godfather Part II*, a torch passed between two generations of method actors. But where Brando, James Dean and Montgomery Clift feminized male screen acting with their techniques for harnessing interior feelings, a series of uncompromisingly hard-edged masculine performances in the 1970s made De Niro the archetypal method actor. No level of commitment was too much: from mastering the Sicilian dialect for the *Godfather* sequel, to earning a New York cabbie's licence for *Taxi Driver* (1976), to demanding a live round be in the revolver used in the Russian roulette scene of *The Deer Hunter* (1978). The resulting deep immersion in a gallery of misfits, mopes and mobsters – New Hollywood ably furnishing both him and his rival Al Pacino with these down-at-heel roles – counts as one of the great actorly pursuits of psychological truth. Martin Scorsese gave him his masterpiece role as *Taxi Driver*'s embittered loner Travis Bickle, talking not just to himself but to the post-Vietnam, post-Nixon mood of paranoia and disintegration. Their long collaboration, dormant for most of the 1980s before the two wise-guy triumphs of *Goodfellas* (1990) and *Casino* (1995), ranks among the most important actor–director partnerships in cinema.

3-SECOND TRAILER
Robert De Niro has gone to exceptional lengths to prepare for his roles, making him a legendary method actor.

3-MINUTE SEQUEL
De Niro later exploited his association with mafioso roles for comedy purposes in 1999's *Analyze This*. The spectacle of his panic-attack-stricken mob boss tickled audiences, and ushered in a flippant late-career phase. Flagrantly self-parodic films such as *Meet the Parents* (2000) courted the box office as hard as they dispirited admirers of his once-ascetic acting creed and hardcore quality control.

RELATED FEATURES
See also
GANGSTER MOVIES
page 40

NEW HOLLYWOOD
page 108

3-SECOND BIOGRAPHIES
STELLA ADLER
1901–92
Leading teacher of the Method, who tutored De Niro, Marlon Brando, Elizabeth Taylor and many others

AL PACINO
1940–
De Niro's fellow method-acting acolyte and 1970s rival; the pair first shared screen time in operatic 1995 thriller *Heat*

MARTIN SCORSESE
1942–
Director who gave Robert De Niro his first significant role in 1973's *Mean Streets*. The pair never looked back

30-SECOND TEXT
Phil Hoad

De Niro brought his uncompromising approach to **Taxi Driver** *and* **Raging Bull.**

SHAH RUKH KHAN
1965–

the 30-second feature

3-SECOND TRAILER

Relying on raw charisma because of his lack of family connections (unusual for Bollywood), this self-made superstar has built himself into India's biggest film brand.

3-MINUTE SEQUEL

Shah Rukh Khan is often cited as the world's most popular film star – something difficult for Western audiences to accept. It's not such an implausible claim when you consider that Bollywood sells far more tickets domestically than Hollywood does (2.2 billion in 2016, against 1.3 billion). Granted, Hollywood still maintains its stranglehold over the global box office, but Bollywood has an invisible reach – distributed on pirated media across the developing world – that is hard to fathom.

Following Bollywood's stagnant 1980s, Shah Rukh Khan emerged as part of a new generation of high-wattage stars in the 1990s. His vast fan base makes the New Delhi-born heart-throb India's closest thing to Tom Cruise, but his genial everyman presence gives him a touch of Tom Hanks. The 1995 rom-com *Dilwale Dulhania le Jayenge* (DDLJ), the country's longest-running film ever, still on theatrical release 20 years after it was made, established him as Bollywood's top romantic lead for a decade. As he cemented his box-office dominance in the 2000s, 'King Khan' also expanded the aspirations and economic potential of Hindi cinema. More playful and westernized than the 'angry young men' in which Amitabh Bachchan once specialized, Khan's roles were lapped up by the Indian diaspora. Pioneering the use of foreign pre-sales to recoup budget outlay, they were designed to do so. Movies such as 2004's *Swades*, in which Khan played a NASA scientist who returns to Uttar Pradesh, and 2010's *My Name Is Khan*, a kind of post 9/11 *Forrest Gump*, confirmed his cross-cultural appeal and furthered Bollywood's global reach. A few bloated blockbusters too many have tarnished the brand in the 2010s, but Khan remains a potent box-office draw.

RELATED FEATURES

See also
ROM-COMS
page 30

MUSICALS
page 38

SATYAJIT RAY
page 56

3-SECOND BIOGRAPHIES

YASH RAJ CHOPRA
1932–2012
Bollywood director who discovered Khan and whose son Aditya has worked with Khan many times

SALMAN KHAN
1965–
Actor; box-office rival to Khan who targets India's Muslim audience with his Eid blockbusters

KAJOL
1974–
Actress; Khan's screen partner in *DDLJ* and six subsequent films

30-SECOND TEXT
Phil Hoad

Self-made film icon 'King Khan' has a versatile range and wide appeal.

CATHERINE DENEUVE
1943–

the 30-second feature

RELATED FEATURES
See also
FRENCH NEW WAVE
page 106

ARTHOUSE CINEMA
page 138

3-SECOND TRAILER
Renowned for playing beautiful ice queens, Catherine Deneuve's long career includes a selection of hypnotic performances for the finest European arthouse directors.

3-MINUTE SEQUEL
To encounter one of her finest performances, check out Francois Truffaut's *The Last Metro* (1980), in which the elegant Deneuve stars opposite another Gallic acting legend: Gérard Depardieu. She plays the star of a theatre troupe in Nazi-occupied Paris, attempting to hide her Jewish husband while putting on regular shows for the public.

Recognized both as a French national treasure and a film icon, Catherine Deneuve has had a long and varied career as an actress. Her first role was in the whimsical Jacques Demy musical *The Umbrellas of Cherbourg* (1964). That film brought her international recognition, and she went on to work with Roman Polanski in *Repulsion* (1965), in which she moulded her aloof persona as a repressed young woman whose sexual fear of men expresses itself in increasing psychosis. Her appearance never suggested the free sexuality of Brigitte Bardot, but a remote glamour – an untouchable quality that appealed to many directors of the time. Deneuve's icy beauty was also used to great effect by Luis Buñuel in *Belle du Jour* (1967), where she is a bored housewife who moonlights as a high-class prostitute. She worked with Buñuel again in the haunting *Tristana* (1970). Deneuve was also cast as a criminal accomplice in *Un Flic* (Jean-Pierre Melville 1972), and in two consecutive roles for Francois Truffaut. In later life she has worked with indie auteurs including Lars Von Trier, Arnaud Desplechin and François Ozon. As she continues to give fascinating performances, Deneuve's reputation as a *grande dame* of French cinema is assured.

3-SECOND BIOGRAPHIES
LUIS BUÑUEL
1900–1983
Spanish surrealist film director

JACQUES DEMY
1931–1990
French director whose films often featured music and fairy tales

30-SECOND TEXT
Christina Newland

Catherine Deneuve debuted in **The Umbrellas of Cherbourg** *before going on to build an impressive arthouse CV.*

MOVEMENTS

Academy Awards American awards for excellence in commercial cinema, which began in 1929. The awards are voted for by members of the Academy of Motion Picture Arts and Sciences and handed out at a lavish televised ceremony. As they are considered the most influential film prizes in the world, a win can make a huge difference to the winner's career or the prestige of a film or studio.

Cinématographe Invented by Auguste and Louis Lumière in 1895, this device could both record and project moving images. The name was coined by inventor Léon Bouly for a previous invention and is derived from a Greek phrase meaning 'writing in movement'. The Lumière brothers bought the right to the name for their own creation.

continuity editing Principles first established in silent-era Hollywood to maintain temporal and spatial continuity, including shot-reverse-shot patterns, establishing shots and the 180-degree, which keeps the camera on one side of a straight line.

film noir Term used by French critics to describe US thrillers made roughly in the period 1944–54. They were characterized by menace, cynicism, low-key lighting and the presence of a *femme fatale* – a mysterious woman who drew the male hero towards danger. The genre spawned its own distinct imitators: 'neo noir' films from 1960 that updated the form.

French New Wave Also known as *La Nouvelle Vague*, this movement in French cinema of the 1950s and 1960s involved a group of young directors including Jean-Luc Godard and François Truffaut. Rejecting literary influences in favour of purely cinematic techniques, and using new lightweight cameras, the New Wave films were youthful, experimental and sometimes political, often using location shooting and authorial commentary. Other New Waves in Britain and Czechoslovakia followed similar principles.

German Expressionism Early twentieth-century art movement, encompassing visual arts, literature, theatre, cinema and even architecture, which privileged psychological realism over verisimilitude. Expressionist works are characterized by simple shapes, visible brush strokes, steep angles and deep shadows. The first German Expressionist film was *The Cabinet of Dr Caligari* (1920).

Hays Code Informal name for the Motion Picture Production Code, Hollywood's first attempt at self-censorship, named after its author Will H. Hays. Technically voluntary, the code gave guidelines for the depiction of topics including sex, profanity, violence, crime and drugs.

Italian Neorealism Group of films made in post-war Italy by directors including Luchino Visconti, Roberto Rossellini and Vittorio de Sica. Their films featured working-class characters, non-professional actors, location shooting and stories of poverty and oppression in Italian society.

method acting Russian actor and director Konstantin Stanislavski developed this influential approach to performance in the early twentieth century, and it was further popularized by Lee Strasberg and his colleagues at the Actors Studio in New York in the 1950s. Often described as an actor's total immersion in a character, method acting is a way for a performer to find a deep emotional identification with a particular role. Marlon Brando, Marilyn Monroe and Dustin Hoffman are famous cinema method actors.

New Hollywood This movement dates roughly from the late 1960s to the early 1980s, and comprises the work of a generation of US film-makers influenced by world and arthouse cinema.

Palme d'Or The most prestigious prize awarded at the Cannes Film Festival, for the best film shown in the main competition. It is regarded as the arthouse equivalent of the Academy Award for Best Picture.

realism This term has two meanings in cinema. Firstly, it is a measure of verisimilitude, or how closely the cinematic image mimics the real world, as in Classical Hollywood cinema. Secondly, it applies to cinema that questions the contrivances that create that illusion: by using only natural light, for example, or by drawing attention to the way that the film is edited.

studio system During the Golden Age of Hollywood, major studios thrived thanks to a combination of factory-inspired production methods, using creative staff on long-term contracts, and vertical integration, that is, the ownership of distribution and exhibition. Anti-trust laws were first used to challenge this monopoly in the late 1940s, leading to the demise of the system by the 1960s.

GERMAN EXPRESSIONISM

the 30-second feature

Murderous sleepwalkers, out-of-control golems, neurotic pianists – just a few of the hallmarks of one of the most influential film movements ever, which erupted out of the subconscious of post-First World War Germany. Drawing on parallel trends in art and theatre, cinema's Expressionists employed heavily stylized sets and lighting and exaggerated acting to convey the destabilizing forces and extreme psychological states bubbling beneath society's surface. The distorted city streets and jagged shadows that filled the backdrops of 1920's *The Cabinet of Doctor Caligari* wrong-footed and exhilarated audiences. Caligari's insane hypnotist (are the off-kilter visuals a window into his mind or ours?) was typical of German Expressionism's morbid bent. The 25 or so films that followed, directed by the likes of Karlheinz Martin (*From Morn to Midnight*, 1920), F. W. Murnau (*Nosferatu*, 1922) and Fritz Lang (*Dr Mabuse the Gambler*, 1922), dug deeper into the anxieties and political turbulence of Weimar Germany. Lang's 1927 science-fiction statement *Metropolis* capped off this scintillating run – just as these widely exported films were proving influential abroad. Universal's classic horror films, helped by several key German emigrés, fed off their dark preoccupations and peculiar staging, while film noir later purloined the high-contrast visual style.

3-SECOND TRAILER
German Expressionism was the 1920s avant-garde explosion that sent shockwaves around the world – and its enthralment with dark impulses foreshadowed Nazi Germany.

3-MINUTE SEQUEL
In order to shape the horror genre, Hollywood made a direct infusion of German Expressionism. Karl Freund, cinematographer on both *The Golem* (1920) and *Metropolis*, imported his unsettling powers to the USA for 1931's *Dracula* and, a year later, as director of *The Mummy*. Paul Leni, known for the 1924 anthology *Waxworks*, became a key director in the late-1920s flurry of pioneering Universal Studios chillers. Fritz Lang, meanwhile, graduated into a major figure of US film noir.

RELATED FEATURES
See also
SILENT CINEMA
page 18

HORROR
page 34

FILM NOIR
page 100

3-SECOND BIOGRAPHIES
ROBERT WIENE
1873–1938
Director who inaugurated German Expressionism with *Dr Caligari*, shot in three weeks, and also contributed 1923's *Raskolnikow*

FRITZ LANG
1890–1976
Monocle-wearing tyrannical director who made four major Expressionist films: *Destiny* (1921), *Dr Mabuse the Gambler*, *Die Nibelungen* (1924) and *Metropolis*

30-SECOND TEXT
Phil Hoad

Distorted perspectives and ominous gloom were hallmarks of German Expressionism.

SOVIET MONTAGE

the 30-second feature

Following the 1917 Russian Revolution, cameras, projectors and even film itself were in scarce supply. However, ideas about the potential for film, both as an art and as revolutionary propaganda, were bountiful. From Vladimir Lenin's belief that 'of all the arts the most important for us is the cinema', to the formal creativity of film-makers including Dziga Vertov, Vselovod Pudovkin, and Sergei Eisenstein, the Soviet Union was ready to reinvent the young medium. Inspired in many ways by the fast cutting of Hollywood movies, Soviet film-makers emphasized editing, or montage – what Eisenstein called 'the nerve of cinema' rather than image or narrative. It was a wholly cinematic technique, not borrowed from art or literature. Soviet montage films used rapid cuts and the collision of images to create dramatic tension and insert new ideas. The fast edits in Eisenstein's *Battleship Potemkin* (1925) underline the violence of revolt, and pass comment on the action, as when inserted shots of lion statues (one sleeping, one sitting, one standing), symbolize the people rising against their oppressors. Vertov's *Man With a Movie Camera* (1929) captured what he called 'film truth' from a collage of fragments of urban life, edited together in impossible or confusing patterns.

3-SECOND TRAILER
Dynamic and revolutionary, the clashing images of Soviet films in the 1920s fashioned a new, exciting form of cinema.

3-MINUTE SEQUEL
The Kuleshov effect is named after an experiment by Soviet film-maker Lev Kuleshov. He edited a close-up of the impassive face of an actor with images of food, a dead girl and a woman on a bed. While each close-up was the same, audiences were impressed by the actor's performance of hunger, grief or desire in each vignette. Kuleshov concluded that the edit creates a new meaning.

RELATED FEATURE
See also
SILENT CINEMA
page 18

3-SECOND BIOGRAPHIES
ALEKSANDR DOVZHENKO
1894–1956
Screenwriter and director, celebrated for his Ukraine trilogy (1928–30)

ESFIR SHUB
1894–1959
Film-maker and editor who pioneered the compilation film, made entirely from existing footage

SERGEI EISENSTEIN
1898–1948
Film director and theorist who pioneered montage in the silent era and made historical epics in the 1930s and 1940s

30-SECOND TEXT
Pamela Hutchinson

Even the pacy editing of Hollywood movies was no match for the rapid, clashing edits of the exhilarating Soviet montage cinema.

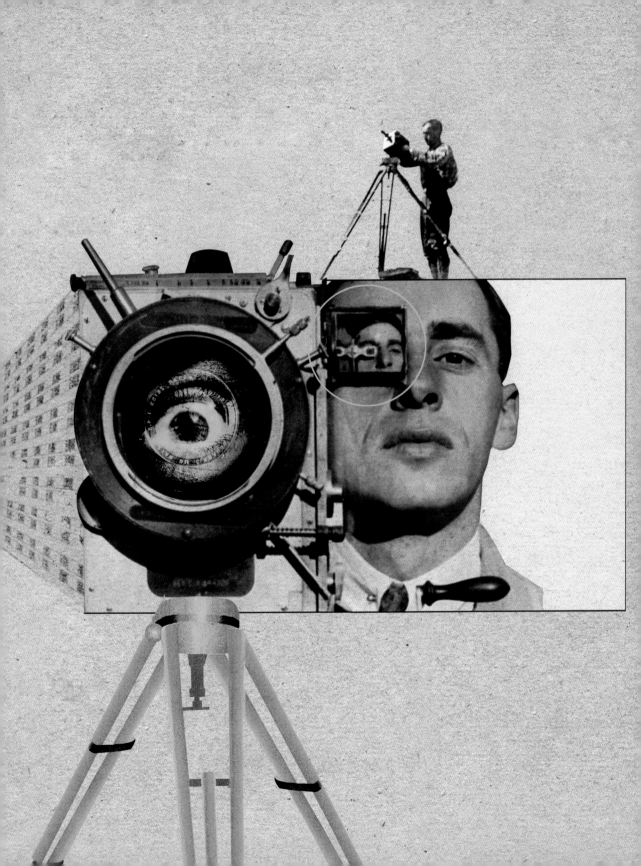

PRE-CODE HOLLYWOOD

the 30-second feature

Referring to the brief years

between the introduction of film censorship and its actual enforcement, the saucy, freewheeling US film industry of 1930–34 has been dubbed 'Pre-Code'. Moralistic censor Will H. Hays helped to write the Production Code that was adopted in 1930 but remained unenforceable until 1934, when religious groups threatened to boycott Hollywood. After that, criminals had to be punished, adulterers corrected, legs and cleavage covered and moral rectitude established. But in those four years, Pre-Code Hollywood was a free-for-all. Pre-Code films often featured fledgling stars such as James Cagney, Mae West, Bette Davis and Barbara Stanwyck and included gangster tales in gritty urban settings as well as melodramas. The naughty spirit of these movies meant that the dialogue could simmer with sexual intrigue, but also that the films could handle remarkably taboo subjects. In *Design for Living* (1933), a woman decides to live in a ménage-à-trois; in *The Public Enemy* (1931), glamorous bootlegger James Cagney tears across the screen. Stanwyck sleeps her way to the top in *Baby Face* (1933) while Ruth Chatterton turns to prostitution in *Frisco Jenny* (1932). Still, it's Mae West in *I'm No Angel* (1933) who sums up the era best: 'When I'm good, I'm very good. But when I'm bad, I'm better.'

3-SECOND TRAILER
Zippy, suggestive and deliriously good fun, Pre-Code Hollywood features movie legends at their wittiest and sexiest – not to mention wearing some fantastically revealing clothes.

3-MINUTE SEQUEL
Pre-Code films are worth seeking out, as they are indelible proof that Old Hollywood was more than capable of rolling in the mud. Some, including *An American Tragedy* (1931) and *Heroes for Sale* (1933), are also revolutionary in the way they broach taboo topics and social problems, such as prostitution, drug use, poverty and abortion. These are some of the most liberal American films of the first half of the twentieth century.

RELATED FEATURES
See also
GANGSTER MOVIES
page 40

THE STUDIO SYSTEM
page 116

3-SECOND BIOGRAPHIES
MAE WEST
1893–1980
A writer, comedienne and sex symbol of 1930s Hollywood; her films prompted a push for censorship but also saved Paramount Studios from bankruptcy

WILLIAM A. WELLMAN
1896–1975
A prolific Golden Age Hollywood film-maker with a set of brilliant Pre-Code releases, including *Night Nurse* (1931) and *Frisco Jenny*

30-SECOND TEXT
Christina Newland

Movie legends such as Mae West, Jean Harlow and James Cagney were at their witty, sexy best in the permissive Pre-Code era.

FILM NOIR

the 30-second feature

RELATED FEATURES
See also
ALFRED HITCHCOCK
page 54

GERMAN EXPRESSIONISM
page 94

Tough, cynical private eyes, slinky, double-crossing dames, and shadowy, geometric lighting? You're definitely watching a film noir. The highly influential trend in American cinema encompasses the stylish crime and detective films that were released from the mid-1940s and well into the 1950s. Beginning roughly with *The Maltese Falcon* (1941) and continuing with adaptations of hard-boiled crime novels such as *Double Indemnity* (1944) and *The Big Sleep* (1946), film noir had a few striking characteristics. Influenced by German Expressionism and using its famous tilted angles and long shadows, noir was a dark reflection of changing morals in a drastically altered world. As a generation of war-weary men returned home, this cycle of films reflected a relentlessly cynical attitude and disinterest in old-fashioned heroism, instead lurking in the dive bars and underbellies of urban haunts with hucksters, crooks and dirty cops. Women were untrustworthy *femmes fatales*, and society seemed to be coming apart at the seams. As the years progressed, film noir seemed to become increasingly violent and nihilistic, culminating in films such as the apocalyptic *Kiss Me Deadly* (1955) and *Touch of Evil* (1958). The rise of television helped to end the film noir era, but it had a big impact on the film-makers and critics of the following generation.

3-SECOND TRAILER
The existential, doom-haunted world of film noir fitted with the gloomy atmosphere following the Second World War and focused on the criminal underbelly of society.

3-MINUTE SEQUEL
Some of the finest noirs were notably made by émigré directors who had escaped persecution or the Nazi occupation in Europe. These included Billy Wilder (*Double Indemnity*, 1944, *Sunset Boulevard*, 1950), Otto Preminger (*Laura*, 1944, *Where the Sidewalk Ends*, 1950), Max Ophüls (*The Reckless Moment*, 1949) and Robert Siodmak (*The Killers*, 1946). This partly accounts for the impact of German Expressionism on film noir, and also for the dark, fatalistic mood of these directors' works.

3-SECOND BIOGRAPHIES
RAYMOND CHANDLER
1888–1959
Prolific author of pulp crime novels adapted for the screen featuring legendary private detective Philip Marlowe, including *The Big Sleep* and *Murder, My Sweet* (1944)

ROBERT SIODMAK
1900–73
German emigré director known for his sleek, stylish crime films and noirs, including *The Killers* (1946) and *Phantom Lady* (1941)

30-SECOND TEXT
Christina Newland

Cynical, criminal and very sexy . . . Humphrey Bogart and Lauren Bacall register a sizzling chemistry in Howard Hawks' influential film noir The Big Sleep.

ITALIAN NEOREALISM

the 30-second feature

3-SECOND TRAILER
The documentary-style realism and overwhelming humanity of Italian Neorealism was a huge influence on world cinema; it would change Italian, French, British and American cinema forever.

3-MINUTE SEQUEL
Italian Neorealism kickstarted the careers of film-makers who became internationally celebrated in the 1960s, including Federico Fellini, Luchino Visconti, Francesco Rosi, Michelangelo Antonioni and Elio Petri. Although few still operated in the strict aesthetic terms of Neorealism, their varied and lively films of that decade – from *L'avventura* (1960) to *8½* (1963) – contributed to what is commonly called Italian cinema's Golden Age.

In the wake of the Second World War, Italy was a nation reeling from bomb devastation, not to mention grappling with the aftermath of Fascism. Most of the famous Roman film studio Cinecittà had been destroyed by enemy attacks, and so a group of ambitious film-makers took to the ruined city streets to baptize a brand-new kind of Italian cinema. Making use of on-location shooting and non-actors, they took as their subjects the genuine issues of the time: the scars of the recent past, hunger and unemployment among working people, and the desperation of poverty and oppression. In the period of roughly 1943–50, the influence of this new, raw film-making was widely felt across the Italian film industry, and was imitated in other countries. Directors such as Roberto Rossellini dealt with the recent German occupation in his Neorealist masterpiece *Rome Open City* (1945) and Vittorio De Sica with the urban poor with *Bicycle Thieves* (1948). Utilizing small cameras and seeking natural lighting, Neorealism demanded emotional honesty and often presented a strong viewpoint on politics and society rather than artifice or drama. The result was piercing and poignant cinema about the post-war conditions of the country, which was universal enough to become a touchstone for film-makers around the world.

RELATED FEATURES
See also
FRENCH NEW WAVE
page 106

NEW HOLLYWOOD
page 108

3-SECOND BIOGRAPHIES
VITTORIO DE SICA
1901–74
Italian film star and director best known for his films *Bicycle Thieves* and *Umberto D* (1952); a key figure in Neorealist cinema

ROBERTO ROSSELLINI
1906–77
Italian film director whose absorbing and tragic War Trilogy, including *Rome Open City*, brought international attention to the Neorealist movement

30-SECOND TEXT
Christina Newland

In postwar Italy, directors including Luchino Visconti and Roberto Rossellini reinvented the language of film realism.

JAPAN'S GOLDEN AGE

the 30-second feature

3-SECOND TRAILER
As the post-war occupation of Japan came to an end in the early 1950s, the country's film industry suddenly captured the world's popular imagination.

3-MINUTE SEQUEL
The Golden Age coincided with a new sense of optimism about Japan's future. Yet it also allowed films such as Kon Ichikawa's *The Burmese Harp* (1956) and Masaki Kobayashi's epic trilogy *The Human Condition* (1959–61) to cast a critical eye on the nation's recent wartime experience, revising the prevailing ideology of imperialist militarism with a decidedly more pacifist outlook that reflected the new mood of the nation.

Ever since the Lumière Brothers' Cinématographe was brought over to Japan in 1897, there had been a flourishing film culture in the country – but it existed in near total isolation, virtually unknown to the outside world. This all changed in the 1950s, now recognized as Japan's Golden Age of cinema, owing to the confluence of two principal factors: Japan finally emerged from wartime deprivation and occupation, and Akira Kurosawa's *Rashomon* (1950) won the Venice Film Festival's Golden Lion in 1951 – the first Japanese film ever to win a major international award. This generated a vogue for Japanese cinema in the West, attracting attention to the latest films by relative newcomer Akira Kurosawa, as well as more veteran film-makers Kenji Mizoguchi, Mikio Naruse and Yasujiro Ozu, who were at the peak of their craftsmanship and seeing their work get foreign exposure for the first time. Loosely adapted from the American film *Make Way For Tomorrow* (1937), Ozu's *Tokyo Story* (1953) offers a calm if confrontational tour of the growing generation gap amid Japan's shifting post-war values, and has gradually acquired status as one of cinema's greatest humanistic achievements. Ishiro Honda's *Godzilla* (1954) captured the anti-nuclear anxieties of the time and engendered a whole new sub-genre of *kaiju* (monster) movies.

RELATED FEATURE
See also
TOSHIRO MIFUNE
page 80

3-SECOND BIOGRAPHIES
KENJI MIZOGUCHI
1898–1956
Japanese film-maker celebrated by Western viewers for his period films of the 1950s

MIKIO NARUSE
1905–69
Director who specialized in pessimistic working-class melodramas with female protagonists; his best-known films, including *Floating Clouds* (1955), were made during Japan's Golden Age

30-SECOND TEXT
Anton Bitel

Japanese cinema enjoyed unprecedented global acclaim in the 1950s, with the impact of great directors and giant monsters.

FRENCH NEW WAVE

the 30-second feature

This fresh-faced, youthful film movement of the late 1950s and 1960s originated with the film critics and enthusiasts who gathered around Parisian movie-houses and bemoaned the state of French cinema. Beginning as writers for the magazine *Cahiers du cinéma*, a group of fledgling film-makers espoused the 'auteur' theory – seeing the director as the artistic 'author' of a film, whose style and themes were prevalent across their output. The best films were ones with a director's personal stamp, evident in visual choices as much as the storyline. The theory's enthusiasts included Jean-Luc Godard, Eric Rohmer, Claude Chabrol and François Truffaut. The latter's low-budget debut feature was called *The 400 Blows* (1959), and based loosely on his own delinquent childhood. Godard soon followed with his landmark *Breathless* in 1960, a fatalistic, percussively edited crime story set on the Paris streets. French New Wave films were characterized by naturalistic and often handheld camerawork, jumpy editing and a loose approach to narrative. Their louche, jazzy style and cool posturing created unforgettable iconography. Although their material was not uniform, they tended to be contemporary and focused on the young generation, whether pop sensations in Agnès Varda's *Cléo de 5 à 7* or criminals on the make in Godard's *Band of Outsiders* (1964).

3-SECOND TRAILER
Innovative, ad-hoc and exciting, films of the French New Wave became critical landmarks and their sprightly 1960s spirit was as influential as it was chic.

3-MINUTE SEQUEL
Two different schools make up the French New Wave movement: the *Cahiers* group and the 'Left Bank' group. The Left Bank group included Agnès Varda (*Cléo de 5 à 7*, 1962), Alain Resnais (*Last Year at Marienbad*, 1961) and Chris Marker (*La Jetée*, 1962), and tended to be older, more studiously left-wing and intellectual. The films lean towards the literary and avant-garde, but several were international arthouse successes.

RELATED FEATURES
See also
AGNÈS VARDA
page 60

CRITICISM
page 122

ARTHOUSE CINEMA
page 138

3-SECOND BIOGRAPHIES
JEAN-LUC GODARD
1930–
One of the founding thinkers and film-makers of the French New Wave, who went on to more radical non-narrative styles in the late 1960s and 1970s

FRANÇOIS TRUFFAUT
1932–84
Director and producer who was a founder of French New Wave; became famous in 1959 after directing *The 400 Blows*

30-SECOND TEXT
Christina Newland

Hip, youthful and innovative, the films of the French New Wave are massively influential.

NEW HOLLYWOOD

the 30-second feature

3-SECOND TRAILER
Reflecting the spirit of a
pessimistic but vibrant era,
New Hollywood produced
subversive and permissive
films, including classics
such as *Midnight Cowboy*
and *The Godfather*.

3-MINUTE SEQUEL
The birth of the blockbuster
era, with simpler, more
spectacle-based films such
as *Star Wars* (1977), is seen
as the end of New
Hollywood and its
downbeat works. In the
wake of the Watergate
scandal and the loss of the
Vietnam War in the 1970s,
US audiences seemed to
grow sick of politically
oriented film-making. By the
1980s, escapism was king.

In the late 1960s and early 1970s,
as hippiedom went sour, a 'new wave' of
Hollywood filmmakers enlivened American
film-making. Youthful directors, obsessed with
European cinema and inclined towards anti-war,
counterculture attitudes, set the world alight
with their subversive takes on American
establishment values. Borrowing from the more
philosophical styles of the French New Wave
and combining them with thoroughly American
concerns, these films introduced the world to
the great directors of the 1970s: Terrence
Malick, Hal Ashby, Francis Ford Coppola, Martin
Scorsese and others. At a time when the studio
system was in financial trouble and box-office
numbers were falling, a series of successful
youth-oriented films – *Bonnie and Clyde* and
The Graduate in 1967, and *Easy Rider* in 1969 –
found a new audience. The films were characterized
by a hip, elliptical editing style, rock soundtracks
and permissive attitudes towards sex and
violence on screen. They were peopled by a
fresh crop of young actors such as Robert De
Niro, who exuded earthy realism and made for
a totally different type of Hollywood film.
Everything from the road movie (*Vanishing
Point*, 1971) to the western (*McCabe & Mrs.
Miller*, 1971) was rethought and most genres
produced at least one masterpiece.

RELATED FEATURES
See also
ROBERT DE NIRO
page 84

FRENCH NEW WAVE
page 106

THE STUDIO SYSTEM
page 116

3-SECOND BIOGRAPHIES
FRANCIS FORD COPPOLA
1939–
New Hollywood film-maker
who interrogated American
myths; director of *The
Godfather* (1972), *The
Conversation* (1974) and
Apocalypse Now (1979)

AL PACINO
1940–
Method actor with a gruff,
realistic style; he grew very
popular in the 1970s with New
Hollywood filmmakers – great
roles of the decade included
Serpico (1973), *Dog Day
Afternoon* (1975) and *The
Godfather* (1972)

30-SECOND TEXT
Christina Newland

**Bonnie and Clyde
*ushered in a new,
subversive era of
American film-making.***

1963
Born Quentin Jerome Tarantino in Knoxville, Tennessee, USA

1987
Makes first feature, *My Best Friend's Birthday*

1991
Attends Sundance Institute Film Lab with short film *Reservoir Dogs*; the feature length version is released two years later

1994
Pulp Fiction plays Cannes Film Festival and wins the Palme d'Or

1995
Tarantino wins Best Screenplay Oscar for *Pulp Fiction*, which is nominated for seven Academy Awards

2010
Christoph Waltz wins Best Supporting Actor Oscar for Tarantino's *Inglourious Basterds*, which receives eight nominations

2013
Wins Best Screenplay Oscar for *Django Unchained*, with Christoph Waltz again winning Best Supporting Actor

2015
Receives a star on the Hollywood Walk of Fame

QUENTIN TARANTINO

It's difficult to think of a modern-day director as immersed in popular film culture as Quentin Tarantino. After exploding on to the scene in the early 1990s, his ability to bring his own sensibility to established genres has seen him evolve from rule-breaking *enfant terrible* to bankable, award-winning, big-budget director. After writing and directing the unfinished short *Love Birds In Bondage* (1983) and little-seen feature *My Best Friend's Birthday* (1987), the 28-year-old took part in the Sundance Film Institute's 1991 Film Lab with short film project *Reservoir Dogs*. It got the attention of up-and-coming producer Harvey Weinstein, who released the feature-length *Reservoir Dogs* through his company Miramax the following year. Despite a strong cast including Harvey Keitel and Tim Roth, and good reviews, the gritty ensemble crime drama failed to set the box office alight – although it has become a cult favourite.

It was enough, however, for Miramax to acquire Tarantino's sophomore screenplay, a multi-strand tale of hapless hitmen, mobsters and boxers. While every major studio had passed on *Pulp Fiction* (1994) because of its violence, Weinstein appreciated Tarantino's vision. The pair had something of a stand-off over Tarantino's decision to cast flat-lining actor John Travolta in the lead role. But Tarantino

prevailed, and his casting of stars who had hitherto fallen out of favour – such as Pam Grier in *Jackie Brown* (1997) and Kurt Russell in *The Hateful Eight* (2015) – has become a trademark. While the film is a bravura piece of storytelling, taking unlikely inspiration from Jean-Luc Godard, Weinstein's release strategy guaranteed its success. The plan was to make it a must-see event, a number of carefully planned screenings building early word-of-mouth publicity before a glitzy showcase at Cannes, where it sensationally won the Palme d'Or. A targeted awards campaign then achieved seven Oscar nominations, including Best Picture, and secured Tarantino his first win for Best Original Screenplay.

This combination of creative talent and business acumen kick-started the US film industry, which had been in a quagmire since the end of the 1980s action boom, and propelled Tarantino into the spotlight. He went on to make a slew of well-received, award-winning films that similarly showcase his eclectic array of influences, from Godard and samurai master Akira Kurosawa to Alfred Hitchcock and spaghetti westerns. While all boast the extreme violence that has become his calling card, his talent as an uncompromising, influential and lucrative film-maker has never been in doubt.

Nikki Baughan

THE BUSINESS

Academy Awards American awards for excellence in commercial cinema, which first began in 1929. The awards are voted for by members of the Academy of Motion Picture Arts and Sciences and handed out at a lavish televised ceremony.

anamorphic process Technique for shooting widescreen cinema using standard 35mm filmstock.

arthouse A cinema that specializes in foreign-language, repertory and art films. Also gives its name to a type of film that rejects mainstream conventions and goal-oriented action in favour of social realism, expressiveness, or an emphasis on imagination and speculation.

Blu-ray An optical disc that can store hours of high-definition video – an upgrade to the DVD (digital versatile disc) first made available to consumers in 2003.

celluloid film Blanket term used for filmstock as opposed to digital recording. Transparent, flexible film stock was first sold by Eastman Kodak in 1889, and had a dangerously flammable nitrate base. Safety stock was introduced in the 1930s and finally replaced nitrate in the 1950s.

cinematography The art and science of photographing moving images. Also known as directors of photography, cinematographers work alongside the director and are responsible for choosing lights, cameras and lenses.

Digital Versatile Disc (DVD) Optical disc that could store far more data or video than previous tape-based formats. First introduced in 1995, its dominance of the home video market was threatened by Blu-ray and streaming services.

Golden Age of Hollywood Roughly defined as 1927–63, the period when US cinema was the dominant form of popular mass entertainment, produced using the processes of the studio system, with techniques and aesthetics now described by the umbrella term Classical Hollywood cinema. With hindsight, critics have discovered much to admire, including touches of individualism and brilliance.

Golden Bear Award given to the best film in competition at the Berlin Film Festival.

Gotham Awards The first prize ceremony of the awards season, the Gothams are awarded to independent films.

Governors Awards Offshoot of the Academy Awards, handed out since 2009 at a separate ceremony to reward lifetime achievement in the cinema.

high-definition Video images with greater resolution than standard definition, for example, much greater than 480 vertical lines in North America and 576 vertical lines in Europe.

IMAX 70mm film format producing moving images of larger size and higher resolution than the standard format. The film runs horizontally rather than vertically through the projector.

Oscar Official nickname for the Academy Awards. The name Oscar was first used in public by Walt Disney in 1932, but there is a dispute over who invented it. Bette Davis claimed in her autobiography that she named the statuette after her first husband, Harmon Oscar Nelson, while others say the Academy's executive secretary Margaret Herrick exclaimed that the figurine looked like her uncle Oscar and the name stuck.

Palme d'Or The most prestigious prize awarded at the Cannes Film Festival, for the best film shown in the main competition. Its prestige means it is regarded as the arthouse equivalent to the Academy Award for Best Picture.

studio system During the Golden Age of Hollywood, major studios thrived thanks to a combination of factory-inspired production methods, using creative staff on long-term contracts, and vertical integration, that is, the ownership of distribution and exhibition. Anti-trust laws were first used to challenge this monopoly in the late 1940s, leading to the demise of the system by the 1960s.

virtual reality (VR) Immersive technology that allows users, often wearing headsets, to explore a realistic three-dimensional environment.

visual effects (VFX) The arts and techniques of adding effects to live-action moving images. The earliest VFX involved in-camera tricks and dyes painted on to the film. Today, filmed images can be manipulated and augmented by computers, a process known as computer-generated imagery (CGI). This technology was once reserved for studios with large budgets but is increasingly accessible to amateur and independent film-makers.

THE STUDIO SYSTEM
the 30-second feature

While Hollywood was not the birthplace of film, it is home to the studio system: a community of huge production houses creating the big-budget blockbusters that dominate the global box office. Moving to the West Coast to escape the oligopoly of the Edison company around New York, industry pioneers began building studios in California from 1913. During Hollywood's Golden Age, eight companies grew to dominance; Fox Film Corporation (later 20th Century Fox), Loew's Incorporated (parent company to Metro-Goldwyn-Mayer), Paramount Pictures, RKO, Warner Bros, Universal Pictures, Columbia Pictures and United Artists. By combining production facilities, distribution divisions, cinema-chain ownership and iron-clad contracts with major stars, they effectively cornered the market. Other studios existed in Hollywood alongside the Big Eight, but their lack of competitive clout was indicated by their collective name of Poverty Row. Other countries had their own vertically integrated studios, such as the UK's Rank Organisation, France's Pathé-Natan and Japan's Nikkatsu, but none reached Hollywood's levels of power and influence. In 1948, a Supreme Court anti-trust ruling forced the separation of production, distribution and exhibition branches, sounding the death knell for the traditional studio system.

3-SECOND TRAILER
From the Golden Age to today's blockbuster era, the Hollywood studio system is the backbone of the film business.

3-MINUTE SEQUEL
While the traditional Hollywood system is no longer in operation, the rise of streaming has brought with it the growth of a new breed of studios. Huge on-demand platforms such as Amazon and Netflix are branching into original film production, with the results made directly available to their massive global audiences without the need for a theatrical release. Their influence and reach are so great that some pundits believe they could change the face of the industry.

RELATED FEATURES
See also
MARY PICKFORD
page 74

NEW HOLLYWOOD
page 108

INDEPENDENT CINEMA
page 118

3-SECOND BIOGRAPHIES
WILLIAM FOX
1879–1952
Founded Fox Motion Pictures in 1915; he bought patents for the Movietone system for recording sound on film in 1926 and lost control of the studio in a hostile takeover in 1930

HARRY COHN
1891–1958
Founded the CBC Film Sales Corporation in June 1918, which became Columbia Pictures in 1924

30-SECOND TEXT
Nikki Baughan

Hollywood's power grew with the rise of the studio system, essentially a factory for film-making, albeit a very glamorous one.

INDEPENDENT CINEMA

the 30-second feature

Traditionally recognized as anything made outside the established studio system, independent cinema has become increasingly diverse in recent years. Affordable equipment together with various financing options – including national and regional grants, crowdfunding (when members of the public give money in return for various rewards) and individual investment – mean that many people with an inclination to make a film can do so. Not every independent film finds an audience beyond the director's social circle, but lots do receive wider distribution. The global film festival circuit is a valuable route to audience for these 'indies', and the pro-active independent film-making community organizes regular international events and awards, such as the Independent Spirit Awards. During the independent boom of the 1990s, when films including Quentin Tarantino's *Pulp Fiction* and Frank Darabont's *Shawshank Redemption* (both 1994) were winning awards and audiences, Hollywood studios began acquiring indie distributors – for example, Disney bought Miramax in 1993 – or opened boutique arms, such as Warner Independent Pictures. However, independent film continues to thrive largely as a welcome counterpoint to the studios' mega-budget franchise model.

3-SECOND TRAILER
There is life outside the big film studios – affordable digital technology and alternative sources of finance keep independent cinema in business.

3-MINUTE SEQUEL
Since they don't have to conform to the risk-averse business strategies of the major studios, which treat cinema primarily as a commercial rather than an artistic endeavour, independent films are freer to push the boundaries of narrative and form. Ironically, however, many independent directors are eventually swallowed up by the studio system; Rian Johnson for example, made indie hits such as *Brick* (2005) and *Looper* (2012) before directing *Star Wars: The Last Jedi* for Walt Disney in 2017.

RELATED FEATURES
See also
FRENCH NEW WAVE
page 106

NEW HOLLYWOOD
page 108

DIGITAL FILM-MAKING
page 130

3-SECOND BIOGRAPHIES
JIM JARMUSCH
1953–
US independent director, actor, writer and composer whose highly distinctive indie movies include *Stranger than Paradise* (1984) and *Paterson* (2016)

STEVEN SODERBERGH
1963–
Acclaimed US director whose independent debut feature *Sex, Lies and Videotape* (1989) won the Palme d'Or at Cannes. He continues to work in and out of Hollywood and in TV

30-SECOND TEXT
Nikki Baughan

Films made outside the big studios can still reach wide audiences.

FESTIVALS

the 30-second feature

Far more than just a chance to roll out the red carpet, the ever-growing international film-festival circuit is an intricate, expertly managed and important business network. The biggest events also run business markets attended by sales agents, distributors and other industry figures and so play host to every stage of the film-making process, from pre-production sales and distribution deals to footage screenings and premieres. Festivals prove an essential stop on the publicity trail for films at all stages of production. Early reviews, photo calls and star interviews often help to generate word-of-mouth buzz months before a film is released. While the grandfathers of the festival circuit are Cannes, Venice and Berlin, there are hundreds of annual events across the globe, with new ones popping up every year. The festival programmes are selected by teams of dedicated and skilled programmers, but submissions are usually open to all films that meet an event's entry criteria. Festival selection can be particularly helpful for independent film-makers, giving them access to audiences and possible awards that can help secure post-festival distribution deals. Festival play is also a helpful litmus test for movies of all budgets; audience feedback allows film-makers to tweak their product if necessary.

3-SECOND TRAILER
The huge network of international film festivals is a valuable industry resource, from the sales and distribution deals that happen behind the scenes to the glamorous red-carpet premieres.

3-MINUTE SEQUEL
With so many festivals crowding the film calendar, it takes careful planning to ensure that each event has a unique identity, and that each film plays in the right place at the right time. The premiere of a hotly anticipated movie is a festival's biggest coup. Many of the year's strongest releases will have done an exhaustive run of the festival circuit before going in front of general audiences.

RELATED FEATURE
See also
AWARDS
page 124

3-SECOND BIOGRAPHIES
GUIDO BRIGNONE
1886–1959
Italian director and winner in 1934 of the first ever-festival prize, Venice's Mussolini Cup, for *Teresa Confalonieri*

JEAN ZAY
1904–44
French Minister for National Education and creator of the Cannes Film Festival; first planned for 1939, but cancelled due to the Second World War and eventually held in 1946

ROBERT REDFORD
1936–
US actor and founder of the Sundance Film Festival, held each year since 1978

30-SECOND TEXT
Nikki Baughan

Behind the glamour of the red carpet and noise of the press junkets, there are important deals to be done on the festival circuit.

CRITICISM

the 30-second feature

Writing about films began in the 1910s, generally in the form of simple notices, but as movies started capturing the popular imagination, appraisals of this relatively new medium grew more sophisticated, in newspapers and specialist journals. In 1928, US critic Irene Thirer introduced the first-ever star rating system to grade films in her reviews for the *New York Daily News*. While such ratings took decades to become the standardized convention that they are today, there has always been an impression (not always borne out in practice), that press criticism privileges evaluation over analysis, interpretation and contextualization. Those last three have certainly been more the focus of academic criticism, which has evolved a theoretical set of terms for cinema's internal mechanics and genre categorizations. This rigorous methodology is also present and correct in at least some film journalism, which has now spread from the printed page to radio, television, websites, blogs and podcasts. Indeed, the democratizing element of the internet has validated the cliché that 'everyone's a critic', even if the paid, professional critic continues to be a much rarer breed. While film critics have always been predicting the end of their craft, it remains in rude health, reading the world through cinema.

RELATED FEATURES
See also
ALFRED HITCHCOCK
page 54

CULT CINEMA
page 150

3-SECOND TRAILER
If films offer snapshots of the world, film criticism equips us to read and talk about those movies.

3-MINUTE SEQUEL
Film criticism is, first and foremost, the province of film-makers themselves, given that their own films inevitably respond to and expand upon the work of predecessors. Conversely, there have been many professional film critics who have gone on to realize their theories on the big screen. Celebrated directors from Jean-Luc Godard to Dario Argento and Park Chan-wook all started out working in film journalism.

3-SECOND BIOGRAPHIES
ANDRÉ BAZIN
1918–58
Renowned French film critic and theorist, co-founder of *Cahiers du Cinéma* in 1951

PAULINE KAEL
1919–2001
Influential US critic for *The New Yorker*, known for her trenchantly contrarian and often personal writing style

ROGER EBERT
1942–2013
US film critic for the *Chicago Sun-Times*; he helped to popularize film criticism on several television shows

30-SECOND TEXT
Anton Bitel

From lone voices, such as Pauline Kael, to the online consensus, we love to rate the movies.

AWARDS
the 30-second feature

The glamour – and clamour – of awards season marks the end of the film year. The red carpets and flashbulbs are, however, just the visible part of a carefully managed system that has its roots in the business of making money. Distributors and studios campaign hard for awards because a nomination or win acts as a recognizable, reassuring stamp of quality for audiences and increases their own standing. The Academy Awards, which have been rewarding cinematic achievement since 1929, remain the holy grail. Producers spend millions of dollars on Oscar campaigns, including distributing the film to voters and taking out 'For Your Consideration' adverts, but it is often money well spent. The Academy Awards ceremony is broadcast in more than 200 countries and success brings with it a huge increase in box-office returns. Oscar-winning stars can also see their salaries increase dramatically; hence their willingness to play along. Other international awards, including those specific to individual festivals, such as Cannes' Palme d'Or and Berlin's Golden Bear, are also essential marketing tools. An award or nomination can be particularly valuable to an independent or arthouse film unable to compete with better-financed competitors, bringing industry and audience attention it may otherwise never have received.

RELATED FEATURE
See also
FESTIVALS
page 120

3-SECOND TRAILER
While audiences enjoy the glamour of awards ceremonies, for the film-makers in the running, a nomination or win is a serious matter.

3-MINUTE SEQUEL
Traditionally beginning with the Governors Awards or the independent Gotham Awards in November and culminating with the Academy Awards in March, each year, awards season is exhilarating for film-makers. Discerning audiences also revel in this period after the summer's blockbuster bombast; during the autumn theatrical window, distributors tend to release their high-quality contenders for awards.

3-SECOND BIOGRAPHIES
CECIL B. DEMILLE
1881–1959
US director of *Union Pacific*, recipient of the inaugural Palme d'Or (then called the Grand Prix) at the 1939 Cannes Film Festival

EDITH HEAD
1897–1981
US costume designer; she was nominated for a remarkable 34 Academy Awards and won eight

MERYL STREEP
1949–
US actress who has won three Oscars and been nominated for more than 20

30-SECOND TEXT
Nikki Baughan

More than just a shiny trophy – a film award can change a career or launch a small film into the stratosphere.

1944
Born George Walton Lucas Jr in Modesto, California, USA

1967
Establishes American Zoetrope with Francis Ford Coppola

1971
Releases his sci-fi debut *THX-1138*, a commercial failure; founds Lucasfilm

1973
Writes and directs *American Graffiti*

1975
Establishes computer effects company ILM

1977
Releases *Star Wars: Episode IV: A New Hope*, the first *Star Wars* movie

1981
Writes and produces first Indiana Jones film, *Raiders of the Lost Ark*, directed by Steven Spielberg

1986
Produces fantasy adventure *Labyrinth*

1992
Recipient of the Irving G. Thalberg Memorial Award for creative producers at the Academy Awards

1999
Directs *Star Wars: Episode I – The Phantom Menace*, in which he trials the first generation of digital cameras

2012
Sells Lucasfilm and ILM to Walt Disney

GEORGE LUCAS

In 1977, *Star Wars: Episode IV: A New Hope*, the third film from US writer and director George Lucas, made its debut and effectively changed the face of the modern movie landscape. While the *Star Wars* franchise remains perennially crowd-pleasing, it was Lucas' innate understanding of the business of film that turned him into one of cinema's most powerful players.

Lucas' ability to play the long game became apparent after he graduated from the University of Southern California in 1967, when he co-founded independent production company American Zoetrope with Francis Ford Coppola. Through that outfit, Lucas made his first film, dystopian sci-fi *THX 1138* (1971), a commercial flop. Undeterred, he founded Lucasfilm and, in 1973, released *American Graffiti*, which received five Academy Award nominations including Best Picture.

That success was enough to inspire 20th Century Fox to produce and distribute Lucas' follow-up project, despite the fact that every other studio had turned it down. *Star Wars* came about because Lucas was unable to obtain the rights to adventure serial *Flash Gordon*. Influenced by his love of samurai films and spaghetti westerns, *A New Hope* was a hit with audiences, becoming the highest-grossing film of that time, winning six Academy Awards and spawning a long-lasting franchise.

That *Star Wars* became such a global cultural phenomenon was largely down to Lucas' decision to forego a higher fee for writing and directing *A New Hope* in favour of retained ownership of licensing and merchandising rights. *Star Wars* games, toys and collectibles were popular from the start and earned Lucas a fortune that he could plough back into producing (and sometimes writing) myriad *Star Wars* sequels and spin-offs, along with franchises such as *Indiana Jones* (created with Spielberg).

Crucially, Lucas was at the forefront of film-making technology as well, founding computer- effects company Industrial Light & Magic (ILM) in 1975. ILM continually pushed the Visual Effects (VFX) envelope and, in 2006, invented the motion-capture technique that subsequently became a blockbuster standard. Lucas was also an early adopter of digital film, and computer animation powerhouse Pixar was a subsidiary of Lucasfilm until it was sold to Apple's Steve Jobs in 1986. Although he sold Lucasfilm to Walt Disney in 2012, Lucas remained active as a consultant on both the *Star Wars* and *Indiana Jones* franchises. The continued success of *Star Wars* films is a testament to Lucas' skills in both business and film.

Nikki Baughan

WIDESCREEN & BEYOND

the 30-second feature

3-SECOND TRAILER
Film-makers are continually trying to break out of the box of the simple square frame by evolving widescreen formats.

3-MINUTE SEQUEL
The most recent iteration of the widescreen idea is virtual reality (VR), with forward-thinking film-makers, festivals and educators increasingly experimenting with fully immersive films that are viewed via an individual headset, and place the audience in the centre of the action. While some pundits believe VR is the future, it remains to be seen whether cinema auditoriums of the future will be full of patrons wearing such headsets.

While 35mm film stock has largely been accepted as the industry standard from the early days of cinema, it has never been the only format in use. Widescreen, defined as any image with a width-to-height ratio greater than 1.37:1, was first used in the late 1890s, although it began to be seen in the late 1920s. The Great Depression of the 1930s necessitated a reduction in production costs, and widescreen formats were rarely used until the 1950s. Then studios developed and patented their own versions of the format in an attempt to lure audiences away from their new television sets. While some, such as CinemaScope, used the anamorphic process, in which a film is shot on standard 35mm with the image stretched into widescreen ratio, the refusal of influential directors including Alfred Hitchcock to use this method resulted in development of more aesthetically pleasing technology, such as VistaVision. An increasing number of films are now being shot in 70mm, which offers four times the image area of standard 35mm, a format that had almost become obsolete thanks to a lack of affordable projectors. Indeed, the need to create a more immersive cinema experience has seen movies grow ever bigger, with IMAX and 3D pushing traditional visual boundaries.

RELATED FEATURES
See also
EARLY CINEMA
page 16

STANLEY KUBRICK
page 52

QUENTIN TARANTINO
page 110

3-SECOND BIOGRAPHIES
ENOCH J. RECTOR
1863–1957
US director of an 1897 documentary depicting a boxing match; shot on 63mm Eastman stock, possibly the first widescreen film

CHRISTOPHER NOLAN
1970–
British director and influential campaigner for celluloid film-making; he shoots regularly in 70mm IMAX, such as for 2017's *Dunkirk*

30-SECOND TEXT
Nikki Baughan

The big screen keeps getting bigger, thanks to the technologies of widescreen, 3D and virtual reality.

DIGITAL FILM-MAKING

the 30-second feature

Think of traditional film-making, and you are likely to bring to mind images of huge whirring cameras, trailing leads and reels of celluloid film. Today, however, most films are made without such cumbersome equipment – the digital revolution has brought lighter cameras and streamlined the entire process. Although the idea of stockless film-making was mooted by Sony in the late 1980s, it didn't catch on until a decade later. The high-definition capabilities and improved portability offered by digital cameras appealed to film-makers; it also made shoots (and reshoots) far less expensive. In 1999 George Lucas announced that, after a successful trial with footage in *The Phantom Menace*, all subsequent *Star Wars* sequels would be shot entirely in high-definition digital format. That not only helped thrust digital film-making into the mainstream, but also saw cinemas begin to replace their traditional projectors with digital versions; a process which has now spread to the majority of theatres. Digital film-making has also contributed to the boom of independent – and specifically very low-budget 'grassroots' – film-making. Affordable digital cameras have democratized production, and mobile technology means that it is now possible to use a smartphone to shoot and edit a film, and to distribute it via online streaming platforms.

RELATED FEATURES
See also
STEVEN SPIELBERG
page 66

INDEPENDENT CINEMA
page 118

WIDESCREEN & BEYOND
page 128

3-SECOND TRAILER
Digital technology has revolutionized film production, making the equipment lighter and the process cheaper.

3-MINUTE SEQUEL
The computerized process of making, producing and distributing films has now been adopted by the majority of film-makers, who celebrate the increased flexibility. Some directors, however, refuse to shoot on anything other than 35mm film, including Paul Thomas Anderson, Quentin Tarantino and Christopher Nolan. The influence of such film-makers has seen the industry move to retain celluloid as a co-existing format, rather than replace it entirely.

3-SECOND BIOGRAPHIES
ANTHONY DOD MANTLE
1955–
British cinematographer who shot Danny Boyle's *Slumdog Millionaire* (2008) mainly in digital, and went on to win the Academy Award for Best Cinematography

SEAN BAKER
1971–
US director of transgender drama *Tangerine* (2015), the first film to be shot entirely on an iPhone

30-SECOND TEXT
Nikki Baughan

A digitally shot film could be a special-effects epic or a small, intimate drama – but the industry has not forsaken celluloid entirely.

HOME VIDEO

the 30-second feature

Film-viewing has traditionally

been thought of as a group activity, but home projectors have been available since the silent era, and during the 1950s many more people began watching films at home. The introduction of Super8 film in 1965 was a marked improvement on the existing 8mm format, but it was extremely expensive and remained niche. A decade later, however, the tide began to turn with the introduction of Sony's Betamax in 1975, and JVC's VHS a year later. Although video cassettes were mostly rented, with cassettes priced too high for individual purchase, distributors soon realized that film fans were interested in owning their favourite movies. This became possible with the introduction of video players. By the mid-1980s, the home-video market was booming and, ten years later, advances in laser technology resulted in the Digital Versatile Disc (DVD). This had greater storage capacity, and so distributors were able to tempt audiences with special content alongside the film. The advent of the higher-definition Blu-ray in 2006 complemented the growing availability of large televisions and high-quality surround sound systems. In the 2010s, the expansion of on-demand streaming platforms such as Amazon and Netflix, which began to produce their own original films, made the living room as popular – and lucrative – as the auditorium.

3-SECOND TRAILER
From the birth of the video cassette in 1975, home entertainment has grown into a hugely profitable industry, with on-demand platforms rivalling the cinema.

3-MINUTE SEQUEL
With an increasing number of people watching movies at home, cinemas have fought back by investing in better seats, dynamic sound and digital projection. The most valuable tactic in the exhibitors' arsenal is, however, the theatrical window – the time between a film's cinema run and its home entertainment release. Traditionally six months, it has been shortened to 90 days, and some films are released simultaneously for cinemas and on-demand platforms. It remains the topic of passionate industry debate.

RELATED FEATURES
See also
INDEPENDENT CINEMA
page 118

WIDESCREEN & BEYOND
page 128

DIGITAL FILM-MAKING
page 130

3-SECOND BIOGRAPHIES
KI-DUK KIM
1934–2017
South Korean director of *The Young Teacher* (1972), believed to be the first film released to the public on VHS (in 1976)

REED HASTINGS
1960–
US co-founder, along with Marc Randolph, of Netflix in 1997; it evolved from renting DVDs by mail into making its own films and TV programmes

30-SECOND TEXT
Nikki Baughan

Do we even need cinemas to enjoy film any more? New technologies have enhanced the home viewing experience.

BEYOND THE MULTIPLEX

BEYOND THE MULTIPLEX
GLOSSARY

cinéma vérité Form of documentary film also known as observational cinema, which allows for more interaction between film-maker and subject, and the possibility of setting up scenarios for the camera.

fleapit Informal name for a cheap, dirty cinema. Fleas were a genuine pest in the days of continuously screened films, as seats were not empty for long and remained warm and welcoming to parasites.

freeze frame Technique whereby the same frame remains on screen, freezing the action. Often used in the endings of films, as in François Truffaut's *The 400 Blows* (1959).

French New Wave Also known as *La Nouvelle Vague*, this movement in French cinema of the 1950s and 1960s involved a group of young directors including Jean-Luc Godard and François Truffaut. Rejecting literary influences in favour of purely cinematic techniques, and using new lightweight cameras, the New Wave films were youthful, experimental and sometimes political, often using location shooting and authorial commentary. Other New Waves around the world followed similar principles.

genre Category of films, such as western, musical and thriller, all with their own tropes and often sub-genres too. Commercial cinema is more likely to slot into a genre than arthouse fare.

grindhouse US term for a cinema that showed exploitation films: those that cashed in on the popular appetite for lurid sex and violence, or trends and niche genres such as biker movies or zombie films. Such movies are now mostly viewed online.

Italian Neorealism Group of films made in post-war Italy by directors including Luchino Visconti, Roberto Rossellini and Vittorio de Sica. Their films featured working-class characters, non-professional actors, location shooting and stories of poverty and oppression in Italian society.

jump cut Abrupt edit that disrupts the narrative flow by 'jumping' forwards in time without moving the camera (or moving it only slightly). It was used in early cinema for trick effects and is now mostly used to call attention to the editing.

New German Cinema Period from the early 1960s to the 1980s when a new generation of film-makers emerged in Germany, including Wim Wenders, Rainer Werner Fassbinder, Werner Herzog and Margarethe von Trotta. The most successful sprang from the arthouse circuit to international acclaim, with a combination of artistic ambition and social critique. Many in the group were signatories to the 1962 Oberhausen Manifesto, which exclaimed: 'The old film is dead. We believe in the new cinema.'

realism This term has two meanings in cinema. Firstly, it is a measure of verisimilitude, or how closely the cinematic image mimics the real world, as in Classical Hollywood cinema. Secondly, it applies to cinema that questions the contrivances that create that illusion: by using only natural light, for example, or by drawing attention to the way that the film is edited.

split-screen Device in which the frame is divided into two or more sections, with simultaneous action in each one.

surrealist The surrealist movement in art dates from the early twentieth century and prioritizes the imagery of the subconscious and dreams over exterior reality.

ARTHOUSE CINEMA

the 30-second feature

Arthouse film, or art cinema, encompasses a broad range of genres but generally refers to artistic ventures in cinema, driven largely by authorial vision and by creative value over profit. Such films are defined by their resistance to commercial appeal and are generally produced outside of the major studios. The film-makers expect a limited release for their movies, which are usually shown in speciality cinemas, aptly known as arthouse theatres. Much of arthouse cinema is experimental and opposes traditional cinematic structure. The techniques of classic experimental films such as Jean Cocteau's *The Blood of a Poet* (1930) and the genre's use of stark realism inspired many Italian Neorealist film-makers. *Obsession* (1943) and *Bicycle Thieves* (1948), like many of the works that emerged from New Wave movements across Europe, are considered quintessential arthouse films. Early in their respective careers (and to varying degrees throughout), auteurs such as Ingmar Bergman (*The Seventh Seal*, 1957), Martin Scorsese (*Mean Streets*, 1973) and John Cassavetes (*Shadows*, 1959), made films that were classified as arthouse, marked by their realism and personal style. Arthouse films frequently inspire a cult following.

RELATED FEATURES

See also
ITALIAN NEOREALISM
page 102

EXPERIMENTAL CINEMA
page 144

CULT CINEMA
page 150

3-SECOND BIOGRAPHIES
JOHN CASSAVETES
1929–89
US actor and film-maker known for his independently produced films and *cinéma vérité*-style of film-making

WONG KAR-WEI
1958–
Chinese director noted for his films' vivid colourful aesthetics and unconventional narrative structure

30-SECOND TEXT
Kelli Weston

Visionary directors such as Jean Cocteau and Ingmar Bergman embody the personal, experimental values of arthouse cinema.

3-SECOND TRAILER
Arthouse film encompasses independent, experimental and often international cinema – movies made outside the mainstream that express the director's personal vision.

3-MINUTE SEQUEL
In the past few decades, arthouse cinema has become conflated with independent cinema, although many well-known directors such as Lars Von Trier and Terrence Malick consistently produce well-financed films that challenge traditional cinematic conventions and intentionally eschew mainstream appeal. Contemporary commercial films often feature many of the same technical and narrative strategies originated by arthouse cinema over the years.

FEMINIST FILM-MAKING
the 30-second feature

Feminist cinema emerged in

response to the shallow depictions of women that dominated film: the objectification of women on screen, frequently reduced to tropes or trophies, which led to Laura Mulvey coining the term the 'male gaze' in 1975. Historically, some film-makers had challenged traditional representations of women as objects of desire – George Cukor's US comedy *The Women* (1939) was entirely populated with women. Yet it wasn't until the 1940s and 1950s, when Maya Deren led the way in experimental cinema, that film-makers began to explore the female psyche. Agnès Varda and actress-turned-director Ida Lupino consistently addressed women's social anxieties in their films, such as pregnancy out of wedlock in Lupino's *Not Wanted* (1949) and infidelity in Varda's *Le Bonheur* (1965). These films were rarely welcomed: Věra Chytilová's controversial film *Daisies* (1966), for example, was banned in her native Czechoslovakia. As such, feminist cinema was often incongruous with the mainstream and remains so in many areas of the world. Haifaa al-Mansour's 2012 film *Wadjda* became the first feature-length film directed by a Saudi Arabian woman. However, many modern feminist film-makers, such as Sofia Coppola, Nancy Meyers and Gina Prince-Bythewood, have enjoyed both commercial and critical success.

3-SECOND TRAILER
Feminist film-makers resist the conventional images of femininity and present the female experience in multi-layered depth.

3-MINUTE SEQUEL
Feminist cinema encompasses a wide breadth of perspectives, although the white female experience is often prioritized. *Losing Ground* (1982) was one of the first feature-length dramas directed by an African-American woman – Kathleen Collins – and was largely overlooked upon initial release. Julie Dash's *Daughters of the Dust* (1991) remains a seminal portrait of black womanhood, which inspired other African-American directors such as Kasi Lemmons and Ava Duvernay.

RELATED FEATURES
See also
AGNÈS VARDA
page 60

EXPERIMENTAL CINEMA
page 144

MAYA DEREN
page 146

3-SECOND BIOGRAPHIES
MARGARETHE VON TROTTA
1942–
German director, a key figure of the New German Cinema movement of the 1970s with films that portrayed complex female relationships

CHANTAL AKERMAN
1950–2015
Influential Belgian director known for films including *Jeanne Dielman, 23, Quai du Commerce, 1080 Bruxelles* (1975), considered a classic of feminist cinema

30-SECOND TEXT
Kelli Weston

Feminist film-makers offer an honest, often controversial, portrait of female life – and some unforgettably brilliant movies.

NEW QUEER CINEMA
the 30-second feature

A term coined by academic

B. Ruby Rich in *Sight & Sound* magazine in 1992 to describe the growing number of independent films concerned with the lesbian, gay, bisexual and transgender experience, New Queer Cinema reflects a growing awareness of sexual identity as fluid and diverse. The genre has become more mainstream over recent years, attracting big stars and winning audiences and awards, but early examples were pioneering creative outliers. Film-makers defiantly presented their LGBTQ protagonists as outsiders and radicals, living on the fringes of society and engaging in often explicit sexual activity. Following the 1980s, when the AIDS epidemic was in full swing, and conservatives Ronald Reagan and Margaret Thatcher governed on either sides of the Atlantic, New Queer Cinema could be seen as a response to the assault on liberal values. Film-makers such as Todd Haynes (*Poison*, 1991), Greg Akkari (*The Living End*, 1992) and Gus Van Sant (*My Own Private Idaho*, 1991) challenged the conventional heterosexual political and cultural structure. As LGBTQ issues became more central to the social discourse, so queer cinema moved towards the middle ground. Later examples, such as Haynes' *Carol* (2015) or Luca Guadagnino's *Call Me By Your Name* (2017), have achieved success at the box office as well as with critics.

3-SECOND TRAILER
Originally radical outsider movies, films about the lesbian, gay, bisexual and transgender experience have since entered the mainstream.

3-MINUTE SEQUEL
Over recent years international queer cinema has taken a particular interest in the experiences of transgender characters, with films evolving from the softly focused and reverential (*The Danish Girl*, 2015, directed by Tom Hooper) to gritty, ultra-realistic takes featuring trans actors, such as Sean Baker's iPhone-shot *Tangerine* (2015) and Brazil's 2018 Oscar winner *A Fantastic Woman*, directed by Sebastian Lelio.

RELATED FEATURES
See also
PEDRO ALMODÓVAR
page 64

INDEPENDENT CINEMA
page 118

FEMINIST FILM-MAKING
page 140

3-SECOND BIOGRAPHIES
DEREK JARMAN
1942–94
British film-maker whose *Edward II* (1991) is one of the films cited by Rich as a forerunner of the New Queer Cinema movement

STACIE PASSION
1969–
US director of lesbian family drama *Concussion* (2013), widely regarded as one of the most influential examples of modern queer cinema

30-SECOND TEXT
Nikki Baughan

From a radical outsider movement to breakouts of award-winning popularity, LGBTQ cinema has changed with the times.

EXPERIMENTAL CINEMA

the 30-second feature

3-SECOND TRAILER
Experimental cinema defies
conventional styles and
storytelling and is generally
produced outside of the
mainstream.

3-MINUTE SEQUEL
Historically, many female
directors seemed to
gravitate towards
experimental films, given
the limited opportunities
for women film-makers
and thinly realized female
characters on screen.
Making films in the 1940s
and 1950s, Maya Deren
has been praised as the
'mother of the avant-
garde'; her films use
experimental techniques
to explore the body and
consciousness. Likewise,
Shirley Clarke in the 1960s,
and Chantal Akerman from
the 1970s until her death,
used experimental films to
tell stories of marginalized
people, largely absent from
mainstream cinema.

Experimental cinema, also called
avant-garde cinema, includes a vast range of
film-making efforts that challenge traditional
cinematic techniques and conventions. Although
experimental films can be distributed for large
commercial audiences, more often these films
are produced through independent means, on
minimal budgets, with small production teams –
and the film-makers expect a limited audience.
The genre emerged in the 1920s as some film-
makers began to resist what were becoming the
standard methods of film-making, such as linear
narratives and editing techniques. Luis Buñuel,
with his friend surrealist painter Salvador Dalí,
wrote and directed the landmark short film *Un
Chien Andalou* (1929): a series of provocative
scenes unconnected by plot. It was the first film
for Buñuel, who would go on to become one of
cinema's most revered directors. That year also
saw the release of the Soviet silent documentary
Man With a Movie Camera, which uses editing
techniques seen as radical at the time: freeze
frames, split screens and scenes played backwards.
In the post-war decades, film-makers such as
Maya Deren and Jonas Mekas continued the
movement. Certain practices of experimental
cinema, such as non-linear narrative, and editing
techniques such as jump cuts and fast cutting,
have found their way into mainstream fare.

RELATED FEATURES
See also
SOVIET MONTAGE
page 96

ARTHOUSE CINEMA
page 138

MAYA DEREN
page 146

3-SECOND BIOGRAPHIES
SHIRLEY CLARKE
1919–97
US director, celebrated for her
award-winning short films and
her 1961 feature-length film
The Connection, a classic of
independent cinema

JONAS MEKAS
1922–
US director considered the
'godfather of avant-garde
cinema'; a prominent figure
who collaborated with Andy
Warhol and Dalí among others

30-SECOND TEXT
Kelli Weston

*The innovations of
avant-garde films that
challenge conventions
can filter through to
studio movies.*

1917
Born in Kiev, Ukraine

1922
Settles in Syracuse, New York with her parents

1942
Marries cinematographer/ photographer Alexander Hammid

1943
Releases *Meshes of the Afternoon*, a seminal effort in avant-garde film-making

1944
Releases her second film *At Land*, which she wrote, directed and starred in, and Hammid filmed

1945
A Study in Choreograph for Camera continues her theme of dance in film using experimenta film techniques

1947
Divorces Alexander Hammid; awarded a Guggenheim Fellowship grant, which finances her studies in Haiti

1953
Produces groundbreaki ethnographic book *Div Horsemen: The Living Gods of Haiti*, about Haitian voodoo rituals

1961
Dies in New York aged

MAYA DEREN

Born Eleanora Derenkowsky,

Maya Deren came from a middle-class Jewish family in Kiev, Ukraine. In 1922, when she was five, anti-Semitic persecution was reaching its zenith, and her family fled to Syracuse, New York, where her father shortened the family name to Deren. She graduated from New York University with a bachelor's degree and Smith College with a master's, both in literature. In 1941, Deren became an assistant to Katherine Dunham, an African-American choreographer. Dunham was also an anthropologist who had carried out extensive fieldwork throughout the Caribbean, where she studied diasporic religion. Her work would influence Deren's own studies of Haitian culture.

Deren became part of the pioneering experimental cinema movement in 1940s Europe that pushed the boundaries of film. With her second husband Alexander Hammid, a photographer and cinematographer, Deren released the experimental short movie *Meshes of the Afternoon* (1943). Deren appears as the mysterious woman in black and Hammid, opposite her, as the hooded man in a dreamy, Surrealist exploration of the subconscious.

The film is hailed as one of the most significant achievements in US avant-garde cinema. Long after silent film had gone out of fashion, *Meshes* featured neither dialogue nor sound until her third husband, musical composer Teiji Ito, added a score to the film in 1952. *Meshes* also contains the beginnings of Deren's fascination with the body and her investigation of it through cinema and choreography throughout her career.

Deren directed and starred in her next film, *At Land* (1944), about a woman washed up alone on a beach, and the film follows her as she encounters various people. The film continues Deren's exploration of the psyche and the body through doubles and striking choreography. Her next film, *A Study in Choreography for Camera* (1945), examined the latter more blatantly. *Ritual in Transfigured Time* (1946) similarly featured dance and *Meditation on Violence* (1948) studied the graceful movements of Chinese dancer Chao-Li Chi. Her fascination with dance led her to Haiti, where she studied voodoo rituals and even adopted the religion. The documentary based on her book, *Divine Horsemen: The Living Gods of Haiti*, was released posthumously by Ito and his wife.

Kelli Weston

ETHNOGRAPHIC CINEMA

the 30-second feature

3-SECOND TRAILER
Ethnographic cinema combines documentary and visual anthropology to record the everyday lives of people around the world.

3-MINUTE SEQUEL
Ethnography has long attracted controversy, due to the representation of its subjects, given that ethnographic film frequently presents oppressed or otherwise colonized cultures from a Western perspective. Senegalese director Ousmane Sembène famously decried the depictions of Africans in ethnographic films, in 1965 accusing Rouch and other ethnographic films of looking at [Africans] like 'insects'. Measures have since been applied to protect the subjects of ethnographic cinema from unethical screen portrayals.

While closely related to documentary, ethnographic cinema principally tends to cover non-Western cultures and communities, and serves primarily as an anthropological exercise, informed by the theories and methods of that discipline. Robert J. Flaherty was credited with creating one of the earliest documentary films, *Nanook of the North* (1922), which follows the lives of an Inuit family in Quebec, Canada, and although it features elements of docudrama, the work is regarded as one of the early inspirations for ethnographic cinema. Anthropologist Félix-Louis Regnault used film to further his research of certain African cultures, and by the 1930s the genre had developed into a tool of anthropology. During the 1950s, thanks to the influence of French film-makers such as Germaine Dieterlen and Jean Rouch, the genre transcended scientific status and began to be recognized for its political and artistic merit. For example, Rouch's highly acclaimed ethnographic film *I, a Negro* (1958) unfolds a week in the life of Nigerian immigrants living in Abidjan, Ivory Coast and combines elements of fiction – dictated by the film's subjects – and documentary. From the 1970s, David and Judith MacDougall rose to become two of the genre's most famous figures and were some of the first to subtitle indigenous languages.

RELATED FEATURES
See also
EARLY CINEMA
page 16

DOCUMENTARY
page 42

MAYA DEREN
page 146

3-SECOND BIOGRAPHIES
MARGARET MEAD
1901–78
American anthropologist, best known for her film *Trance and Dance in Bali* (1952) and for documenting sexuality in South-east Asian cultures

TIMOTHY ASCH
1932–94
Anthropologist and prolific ethnographic film-maker, known for *Ocamo is My Town* (1974) and *The Ax Fight* (1975)

30-SECOND TEXT
Kelli Weston

Can ethnographic cinema maintain a neutral or sympathetic gaze, or will it always be accused of scrutinizing people 'like insects'?

411   17

CULT CINEMA

the 30-second feature

Much as there were always those who preferred what critic Manny Farber called the 'termite art' of cheaper B movies to the conservatism of the main(stream) features with which they used to be paired, there remains a devoted fan base that faithfully worships the 'outsider' films that make an unselfconscious virtue of their own madness or marginalization. These are 'cult' films, defined as much by their fervent, repeat-viewing audience as by their classification-defying content. Their natural screening time is midnight – the time reserved on US television stations in the 1950s for low-budget genre pictures, and the preferred theatrical exhibition slot in the 1970s for films such as Alejandro Jodorowsky's heady western *El Topo* (1970), Richard O'Brien's perverse horror musical *The Rocky Horror Picture Show* (1975) or David Lynch's dreamy infanticidal debut *Eraserhead* (1977). Their natural home has been the 'fleapit', the drive-in, the grindhouse – anywhere but the multiplex. More recently they are found in direct-to-video formats or on the internet. Products of and for the counterculture, these films are often viewed by their fans through the filter of narcotics or irony, while they tend to be dismissed by the uninitiated as amateurish, impenetrable or just too weird and subversive for comfort.

3-SECOND TRAILER
Cinema's equivalent of outsider art, cult cinema lives at the edges of the mainstream and has its own faithful audience.

3-MINUTE SEQUEL
What constitutes a cult film might be its po-faced earnestness (*Reefer Madness*, 1936), transgressiveness (John Waters' films), all-encompassing ambition (Jodorowsky's or Richard Kelly's films), scuzziness (*The Driller Killer*, 1979), heady visual appeal (*Koyaanisqatsi*, 1982), wide-eyed incompetence (*Plan 9 From Outer Space*, 1959) or just an elusive strangeness (*Liquid Sky*, 1982). However, films that try hard to attain cult status do not always succeed (*Snakes on a Plane*, 2006).

RELATED FEATURES
See also
SCIENCE FICTION
page 32

HORROR
page 34

3-SECOND BIOGRAPHIES
ALEJANDRO JODOROWSKY
1929–
Director of difficult-to-categorize films such as *El Topo* that set the personal, the political, the psychological and the cosmic within recognizable genres

JOHN WATERS
1946–
Baltimore-based director whose shocking, transgressive, often hilarious films concern countercultural misfits living beyond the pale on society's outer margins

30-SECOND TEXT
Anton Bitel

Mad or marginalized? Cult cinema defies both classification and propriety while attracting loyal, passionate audiences.

APPENDICES

RESOURCES

BOOKS

Adventures In The Screen Trade:
A Personal View of Hollywood
William Goldman
(Abacus, 1996)

Cinema Studies: the Key Concepts
Susan Hayward
(Routledge, 5th edition, 2017)

Film: A Critical Introduction
Maria Pramaggiore, Tom Wallis
(Laurence King, 3rd edition, 2011)

Film Noir Reader
Ed. Alain Silver & James Ursini
(Limelight Editions, 2004)

Heavenly Bodies: Film Stars and Society
Richard Dyer
(Routledge, 2004)

A Hundred Years of Japanese Film
Donald Richie
(Kodansha International, 2001)

In the Blink of an Eye
Walter Murch
(Silman-James Press, 1995)

Liquid Metal: The Science Fiction Film Reader
Ed. Sean Redmond
(Wallflower Press, 2004)

How to Read a Film
James Monaco
(OUP, 4th edition, 2009)

Making Movies
Sidney Lumet
(Bloomsbury, 1996)

New Queer Cinema: The Director's Cut
B. Ruby Rich
(Duke University Press, 2013)

Nightmare Movies
Kim Newman
(Bloomsbury, 2011)

The Oxford History of World Cinema
Geoffrey Nowell-Smith
(OUP, 1996)

Picture
Lillian Ross
(Faber & Faber, 1998)

*The Red Velvet Seat: Women's Writings
on the Cinema - The First Fifty Years*
Ed. Antonia Caroline Lant & Ingrid Periz
(Verso, 2006)

Reel to Real: Race, Sex and Class at the Movies
bell hooks
(Routledge, 2008)

Shooting to Kill
Christine Vachon
(Bloomsbury, 1998)

The Silent Cinema Reader
Ed Lee Grieveson & Peter Krämer
(Routledge, 2004)

WEBSITES
Cléo
cleojournal.com

Observations on Film Art
www.davidbordwell.net/blog

Roger Ebert's Great Movies
www.rogerebert.com/great-movies

BFI
www.bfi.org.uk/explore-film-tv

The Current film culture magazine
www.criterion.com/current/posts

Film Comment magazine
www.filmcomment.com

Film Studies for Free
filmstudiesforfree.blogspot.com

Pre-code
pre-code.com

Reverse Shot
www.reverseshot.org

Senses of Cinema journal
sensesofcinema.com

You Must Remember This
www.youmustrememberthispodcast.com

NOTES ON CONTRIBUTORS

EDITOR
Pamela Hutchinson is a freelance writer, critic and film historian specializing in silent and classic cinema as well as women's film history. Based in London, she contributes regularly to publications including *Sight & Sound* magazine and the *Guardian* as well as appearing on BBC Radio 4. She is the author of the BFI Film Classic on G. W. Pabst's *Pandora's Box* (BFI Publishing, 2017) and the founder and editor of silent cinema website SilentLondon.co.uk.

CONTRIBUTORS
Nikki Baughan is a film journalist who has been editor of *Film Review* and *movieScope* magazines, and has also written for *Little White Lies*, *Filmstar*, *The List* and *Screen International*. She is a member of Women in Film and TV and the London Film Critics Circle and has reviewed films on BBC radio.

Anton Bitel is a lecturer in Classical languages at Christ Church College, Oxford, and a freelance film journalist. He regularly contributes to *Sight & Sound* magazine, *Little White Lies*, *RealCrime* magazine,

SciFiNow, *VODzilla.co* and *EyeforFilm*, and he also guests on BBC World Service's *The Arts Show*. He specializes in genre films and the cinema of East Asia, and is a member of the Online Film Critics Society and the London Film Critics' Circle.

Phil Hoad writes for the *Guardian*, Al Jazeera and the BFI, and is former film editor of *Dazed & Confused*. He specializes in Hollywood and other film industries in a global context, and lives in Montpellier, France.

Christina Newland is a writer on film, culture and boxing, specializing in 1970s American cinema. She has written for *Hazlitt*, *Sight & Sound*, *VICE*, the *Guardian*, *Little White Lies* and others.

Kelli Weston earned a Master's degree in Film, Television and Screen Media from Birkbeck, University of London and is a contributor to *Sight & Sound* magazine and *The Skinny*. She specializes in contemporary horror cinema and the role of race in American cinema.

INDEX

ACKNOWLEDGEMENTS

The publisher would like to thank the following for permission to reproduce copyright material on the following pages:

Alamy Stock Photo/A F Archive 8, 41, 45, 65, 81, 89, 103, 151; Chronicle 33; cineclassico 129; Collection Christophel 103, / © Charlie Gray 2012 119; Dinodia Photos 87; dpa picture alliance 103; Entertainment Pictures 67, /face to face 69; Everett Collection Inc 23, 41, 51, 53, 61, 81, 97, 105, 141, 145, 146; Granamour Weems Collection 129; Granger Historical Picture Archive 17, 41, 105, 117; INTERFOTO 19; Lebrecht Music & Arts 97; Moviestore Collection Ltd 9, 33, 43, 59, 99, 105, 107, 119, 145, 151; Natasha Lee 117; Photo 12 35, 39, 45, 57, 63, 69, 85, 95, 131, 143; Pictorial Press Ltd 19, 31, 39, 67, 77; Science History Images 149; ScreenProd/Photononstop 54, 101, 119; United Archives GmBH 29, 65, 141; Universal Art Archive 97; World History Archive 95; ZUMAPRESS.com © Globe Photos 77.

Bibliotheque Nationale de France 6, 139.

Biodiversity Heritage Library 83.

Getty Images/Association Frères Lumière/Roger Viollet 15; Bettmann 129, 141; Bob Henriques 123; Claude Huston/Pix Inc./The LIFE Images Collection 103; John Springer Collection 107; Lambert 133; Paramount/Archive Photos 99; Sacha Masour 139; ullstein bild 45; United Artists/Handout 59.

ImageCollect/Globe Photos 29, 33, 39, 45, 53, 143, 151; C City 78; Christine Loss 85, 109; Graham Whitby Boot/Allstar 36; Ipol 139; Rangefinders 53, 67, 83; Roger Harvey 110; Tom Rodriguez 126.

Library of Congress 20, 75, 95, 109, 117, 149.

Old Design Shop 31.

Rex/Shutterstock/Kobal/Institute of Intellectual Development 69; Universal 67.

Shutterstock/3d_man 121; ABC Photo 85; Abert 61; Adriano Castelli 121; Alexander Chizhenok 63; AlexLMX 75; Andrea Raffin 121; Anna Poguliaeva 87; ARTYOORAN 143; baoyan 81; Bardocz Peter 65; blue-bubble 143; Bob Orsillo 33; BokehStore 125; Budai Romi 83; Bykfoto 123; Chuck Rausin 75; Daniele Carotenuto 15; David Franklin 125; dcwcreations 35; dibrova 125; dimair 123; Djem 123; donatas1205 149; Dsdesign 131; DutchScenery 125; Ekaterina Gorenkova 131; Elena Baryshkina 77; Evannovostro 101; Everett Collection 7, 15, 31, 33, 151; Everett Historical 19, 63, 107; Featureflash Photo Agency 125; Filipchuk Maksym 61; Flas100 123; Gwoeii 123; Henrik Lehnerer 85; Henryk Sadura 65; I.Friedrich 139; I.H. LIU 105; Icons vector 23; Ievgenii Meyer 43; IgorGolovniov 105, 119; Ihnatovich Maryia 129; Irtsya 133; Jag_cz 17; javarman 29; Jica 121; Jim Francis 53; Joanne Harris and Daniel Bubnich 61; Kamenetskiy Konstantin 51; KariDesign 67; Kaspri 103; Katrien1 145; Kjersti Joergensen 81; Klavdiya Krinichnaya 131; Kolonko 105; Konstantin Soukhov 119; Kotenko Oleksandr 67; KrikHill 125; Laboko 31; Leon T 133; Lloyd Paulson 151; LVM 141; Macrovector 89; MaraQu 145; Maryna Stamatova 67; mashroom 99; Maxx-Studio 65; medvedsky.kz 133; Michael G Smith 133; mickyteam 105; Mimadeo 35; Monkey Business Images 129; Nataly Reinch 149; natrot 29; Nosyrevy 125; Nutthapong Thammaruksasit 101; oorka 33; Ostariyanov 103; Ovchinnkov Vladimir 75; p-Format 39; pansuang 57; pashabo 133; Pe3k 117; photka 17; Pola36 89; Potapov Alexander 57; Preto Perola 31; prochasson Fredreic 29; PureRadiancePhoto 121; Quaoar 35; Ramona Kaulitzki 39; Rhonda Roth 95; Rita Ko 105; rocharibeiro 57; Rova N 145; Sergey Nivens 43; Skylines 151; snake3d 31; sociologas 65; Sonja Filitz 119; STILLFX 19, 123; Sunward Art 83; Susalmages 35; Suzanne Tucker 133; Tadeas Skuhra 39; Taiga 123; Tanhauzer 125; tone213 41; turtix 117; tuulijumala 125; VectorPic 19; Venzy 61; xpixel 145; Zakharchuk 87; zeffir 45.

United States Marine Corps 119.

Wikimedia Commons/China Crisis CC-BY-SA 3.0 53; GPS 56 CC-BY-2.0 109; Marcin Wichary CC-BY 39, 129; W Schlaier CC-BY 131.

All reasonable efforts have been made to trace copyright holders and to obtain their permission for the use of copyright material. The publisher apologizes for any errors or omissions in the list above and will gratefully incorporate any corrections in future reprints if notified.